DRAMA CLASSICS

The Drama Classics series aims to offer the world's greatest plays in affordable paperback editions for students, actors and theatregoers. The hallmarks of the series are accessible introductions, uncluttered texts and an overall theatrical perspective.

Given that readers may be encountering a particular play for the first time, the introduction seeks to fill in the theatrical/historical background and to outline the chief themes rather than concentrate on interpretational and textual analysis. Similarly the play-texts themselves are free of footnotes and other interpolations: instead there is an end-glossary of 'difficult' words and phrases.

The texts of the English-language plays in the series have been prepared taking full account of all existing scholarship. The foreign-language plays have been newly translated into a modern English that is both actable and accurate: many of the translators regularly have their work staged professionally.

Edited until his early death by Kenneth McLeish, the Drama Classics series continues with his aim of providing a first-class library of dramatic literature representing the best of world theatre.

Associate editors:
Professor Trevor R. Griffiths
Dr. Colin Counsell
School of Arts and Humanities
University of North London

DRAMA CLASSICS *the first hundred*

The Alchemist
All for Love
Andromache
Antigone
Arden of Faversham
Bacchae
Bartholomew Fair
The Beaux Stratagem
The Beggar's Opera
Birds
The Changeling
A Chaste Maid in Cheapside
The Cherry Orchard
Children of the Sun
El Cid
The Country Wife
Cyrano de Bergerac
The Dance of Death
The Devil is an Ass
Doctor Faustus
A Doll's House
Don Juan
The Duchess of Malfi
Edward II
Electra (Euripides)
Electra (Sophocles)
An Enemy of the People
Every Man in his Humour
Everyman
The Father
Faust
A Flea in her Ear
Frogs
Fuenteovejuna
The Game of Love and Chance
Ghosts

The Government Inspector
Hedda Gabler
The Hypochondriac
The Importance of Being Earnest
An Ideal Husband
An Italian Straw Hat
The Jew of Malta
The Knight of the Burning Pestle
The Lady from the Sea
The Learned Ladies
Lady Windermere's Fan
Life is a Dream
The Lower Depths
The Lucky Chance
Lulu
Lysistrata
The Magistrate
The Malcontent
The Man of Mode
The Marriage of Figaro
Mary Stuart
The Master Builder
Medea
The Misanthrope
The Miser
Miss Julie
A Month in the Country
A New Way to Pay Old Debts
Oedipus
The Oresteia
Peer Gynt
Phedra
Philoctetes
The Playboy of the Western World

The Recruiting Officer
The Revenger's Tragedy
The Rivals
The Roaring Girl
La Ronde
Rosmersholm
The Rover
The School for Scandal
The Seagull
The Servant of Two Masters
She Stoops to Conquer
The Shoemaker's Holiday
Six Characters in Search of an Author
The Spanish Tragedy
Spring's Awakening
Summerfolk
Tartuffe
Thérèse Raquin
Three Sisters
'Tis Pity She's a Whore
Too Clever by Half
Ubu
Uncle Vanya
Volpone
The Way of the World
The White Devil
The Wild Duck
Women Beware Women
Women of Troy .
Woyzeck

The publishers welcome suggestions for further titles

DRAMA CLASSICS

THE MARRIAGE
OF FIGARO

by
Pierre-Augustin de Beaumarchais

translated and introduced by
Stephen Mulrine

NICK HERN BOOKS
London
www.nickhernbooks.co.uk

A Drama Classic

This edition of *The Marriage of Figaro* first published
in Great Britain as a paperback original in 2001 by
Nick Hern Books Limited, 14 Larden Road, London W3 7ST

Copyright in the introduction © Nick Hern Books, 2001

Copyright in the translation © Stephen Mulrine, 2001

Typeset by Country Setting, Kingsdown, Kent CT14 8ES
Printed by Bath Press, Avon

A CIP catalogue record for this book is available from
the British Library

ISBN 1 85459 492 3

Introduction

Pierre-Augustin de Beaumarchais (1732-1799)

Beaumarchais draws heavily on his own experience in
recounting the adventures of his great creation, the wily
jack-of-all-trades Figaro, but in truth, the facts of the
author's life so far outstrip fiction as to be scarcely
credible. Born Pierre-Augustin de Caron in Paris in 1732,
Beaumarchais first took up his father's clock-making trade,
and came to notice at the age of 21, through an episode
which typifies his later career. The young Beaumarchais
had invented a new escapement mechanism for watches,
still in use today, and brought it to the attention of the
King's clockmaker, one M. Lepaute, who began passing
it off as his own. Beaumarchais wrote an indignant letter
to the influential newspaper *Mercure de France*, the first of
many public appeals he would make in the course of a
lifelong search for justice, and was duly summoned to
court to explain his device to the King, Louis XV.
Beaumarchais not only won his case, he also won for
himself the position of royal clockmaker, and an entry into
the charmed circle of the court, which he was soon to
exploit further through another of his talents, by giving
the royal princesses lessons on the harp.

Beaumarchais now had his foot on the ladder, and in
1755, a chance meeting with a certain Mme Franquet,
married to an elderly courtier, resulted in Beaumarchais

eventually purchasing the latter's sinecure office, that of *Contrôleur de la Bouche du Roi*, whose ceremonial duties consisted of walking before the King's food with a drawn sword, but whose practical value, to the ambitious Beaumarchais, was incalculable. A year later, Franquet died, and the young Beaumarchais married his widow, assuming charge of her fortune, and also incidentally the title by which he is henceforth known, from one of her properties. Mme Franquet did not long survive her late husband, however, and Beaumarchais found himself embroiled in protracted litigation over her estate.

Around this time Beaumarchais also made the acquaintance of the powerful financier Pâris-Duverney, and in gratitude for Beaumarchais' assistance with one of his projects, through his influence with the royal princesses, Pâris-Duverney offered to manage his finances. Pâris-Duverney was as good as his word, and within a year, Beaumarchais was able to purchase the office of *Secrétaire du Roi*, which carried with it noble rank. Further promotion came in 1763, with his appointment to the post of *Lieutenant-Général des Chasses*, in charge of enforcing the game laws within the King's domains around Paris.

Beaumarchais had already begun work on his first play, *Eugénie*, and had written several sketches, known as *Parades*, for the private theatre of Mme de Pompadour's wealthy husband. In February 1764, however, he embarked on the first of his 'Figaro' exploits, visiting Madrid on business for Pâris-Duverney, but more romantically, to vindicate his elder sister's honour. The unfortunate Lisette had been jilted by a Spanish archivist, one José Clavijo, and Beaumarchais gained access to him by posing as a French literary editor, before confronting him over morning chocolate with a lengthy recital of his crimes. Clavijo was forced to agree to marry Lisette, but promptly went into hiding, claiming Beaumarchais had held a pistol to his head. Beaumarchais then took his case to King Carlos III, and had Clavijo sacked. Beaumarchais' later account of the affair made it a European *cause célèbre*, and even the subject of a play by Goethe.

Beaumarchais spent a long time on *Eugénie*, which was premièred at the Comédie Française on 29 January, 1767, to an initially hostile reception. Swiftly rewritten, however, the play enjoyed fair success, and emboldened Beaumarchais to begin work on a second play, *The Two Friends*, which was premièred on 13 January, 1770, but failed to repeat the success of *Eugénie*. In the interim, Beaumarchais had remarried, to another widow, Madeleine Wattbled, who gave birth to a son in December 1768.

The failure of *The Two Friends* was the least of Beaumarchais' worries in 1770. Madeleine proved to have scarcely more staying power than his first wife, and died in November of that year, taking with her her fortune, which was in the form of an annuity. From a financial standpoint, however, the death of Beaumarchais' guide and mentor, Pâris-Duverney, was an even more serious blow. The two men had drawn up an agreement to legalise their partnership, but the 87-year-old Pâris-Duverney died in July, before its terms could be fully executed, and the old man's heir, the Comte de la Blache, had a near-pathological hatred of Beaumarchais. To the latter's consternation, La Blache claimed not to recognise his great-uncle's signature on the partnership document, with the implication that Beaumarchais must have forged it. The case went to judgment in October 1777, and although Beaumarchais won easily, La Blache took it to appeal, to the so-called 'Maupeou' Parlement, where he had many powerful friends.

The Maupeou Parlement was the recent creation of Louis XV, who had arbitrarily dismissed the troublesome Parlement of Paris, almost the only check on his absolute power, and installed a body of compliant place-men in its stead. Beaumarchais had every reason to fear their judgment, and so it turned out, though his situation was made infinitely worse by the bizarre episode of his quarrel with the Duc de Chaulnes. Quarrel, indeed, is scarcely the word to describe the homicidal attack launched on Beaumarchais by this half-mad nobleman. Beaumarchais had been visiting an actress at the Comédie Italienne, a lady friend of De Chaulnes, and when the latter found out, he stalked Beaumarchais, sword in hand, for an entire day, before attempting to run him through in his own house, where Beaumarchais was saved from death only by the intervention of his servants.

A dispute of this kind, between noblemen, had to be brought before the Tribunal of the Marshals of France, who properly ruled in Beaumarchais' favour, and packed De Chaulnes off to the fortress of Vincennes to recover his wits. However, the upstart Beaumarchais had no shortage of enemies, and a few days later, he too was imprisoned, on a technicality, in the For l'Evêque. The Parlement, meanwhile, had appointed a judicial assessor to review the evidence in the La Blache affair, one Valentin Goëzman. In the practice of the time, both La Blache and Beaumarchais were expected to present their cases in person to the assessor, who would then report to the

Parlement for a ruling. Unfortunately, while La Blache could lobby for support in every direction, Beaumarchais was allowed out of prison for only a few hours each day, and found it impossible to gain access to Goëzman.

People in Goëzman's position routinely expected to be bribed, and it was intimated to Beaumarchais that a payment of 200 gold *louis*, made through Goëzman's wife, would guarantee a consultation with the great man, essential if his plea was to succeed, and the money would be returned, should he lose. With only a few days to go before the hearing, Beaumarchais managed to collect the money, part cash, part in the form of a diamond-studded watch, and duly delivered it to Mme Goëzman, who then demanded an additional 15 gold *louis*, to pay the judge's secretary, she claimed. Beaumarchais finally got his meeting with Goëzman, and was alarmed to find that the judge knew nothing about his case, and appeared to care even less, though he sardonically assured him that justice would be done.

On 6 April, 1773, Beaumarchais' worst fears were realised – the Parlement ruled in La Blache's favour, and Beaumarchais was fined 56,000 *livres*, plus costs. Within days, his house and furniture in the Rue de Condé were sold, and his father and sister evicted, while he still languished in the For l'Evêque. Mme Goëzman returned his 200 gold *louis* as promised, but greed got the better of her, and she kept the 'supplementary' fifteen, denying all knowledge of it when challenged, and counter-charging Beaumarchais with libel. That was to prove the Goëzmans' downfall, and Beaumarchais, with nothing to lose but his liberty, published a series of four brilliant *Mémoires*, detailing every last absurdity of the libel hearing. Beaumarchais' fame spread throughout Europe, and the *Mémoires* were avidly read not only in the streets, but also at Versailles, and the courts of Vienna and St Petersburg, where Catherine the Great instructed her French ambassador to send them to her as soon as they were printed. Goethe even read them aloud at his soirées in Frankfurt.

Unhappily, on 26 February, 1774, the Parlement pronounced judgment against both Beaumarchais and Mme Goëzman, depriving them of their civil rights, a very serious matter. Beaumarchais, indeed, narrowly escaped branding and a life sentence in the galleys. Not surprisingly, his new play, *The Barber of Seville*, which had gone into rehearsal at the Comédie Française the previous year, had to be postponed. Despite the public reprimand he had received, Beaumarchais was almost immediately sent abroad on a secret mission for the King, to suppress a scurrilous pamphlet about to be published in London, on the loose morals of the King's former mistress, Mme Du Barry. Beaumarchais not only succeeded in buying off the author, one Théveneau de Morande, but also recruited him for the French secret service. Alas, on 10 April, three days after Beaumarchais' return to Paris, his royal master well served, Louis XV died of smallpox, and the new king, the twenty-year-old Louis XVI, felt no obligation whatsoever to Beaumarchais on Mme Du Barry's account.

However, word now came to Beaumarchais (from Morande, naturally), that there was another libel going through the press, in both London and Amsterdam, this time on the alleged sterility of Louis XVI's queen, Marie-Antoinette. Once again, Beaumarchais set off for London, bearing a secret authorisation from the King in a gold box on a chain around his neck. His adventures thereafter leave Figaro's in the shade: persuading the blackmailer Angelucci *alias* Atkinson to destroy his English and Dutch editions; chasing him hell-for-leather across Europe, to retrieve the last remaining copy; being set upon by bandits in a forest near Nuremberg; finally making a personal appeal to the Empress Maria Theresa of Austria, the mother of Marie-Antoinette, who promptly placed him under house arrest until his *bona fides* could be verified at Versailles. Historians are divided as to Beaumarchais' credibility in this whole affair, which he narrates in the manner of a picaresque novel, but there is no denying that this fresh clandestine mission did wonders to establish him in Louis XVI's confidence.

On his return to Paris, Beaumarchais was at last able to see *The Barber of Seville* into production. The play opened at the Comédie Française on 23 February, 1775, when it was roundly hissed by the first-night audience; two days later it was re-staged, shorn of an entire act and extensively rewritten, and became an instant success. Beaumarchais was soon on his travels again, however, and in London he visited the House of Commons almost daily, closely attentive to the developing crisis in the American colonies. By the end of the year he was already sending memos to Louis XVI, advising the King on the necessity to support the American rebels. While the French government dared not become involved officially, Beaumarchais was granted a personal loan of two million *livres*, for the purpose of obtaining weapons and supplies for the insurgents, to be shipped across the Atlantic at his own risk. He was then to be reimbursed in goods – rice, tobacco, indigo, etc., as a commercial enterprise.

Beaumarchais obtained his weapons from government arsenals, planning the whole business so meticulously as even to remove the French coat-of-arms from the 200 cannon he bought, along with rifles and ammunition for 25,000 troops. The complexity of the operation was staggering, but the supplies reached the colonists at the beginning of 1777, and beyond any doubt ensured their turning-point victory over Burgoyne's English army at Saratoga later that year. In fact, it has been estimated that the American rebellion could not have succeeded without French support, and that meant Beaumarchais. Unhappily, although the venture almost bankrupted him, the new republic – officially recognised by France in March 1778 – proved extremely niggardly at settling its debts. Not until forty years after Beaumarchais' death were his heirs able to retrieve even a fraction – 800,000 francs – out of the several millions owed to him by the American Congress.

On a happier note, Beaumarchais' civil rights were formally reinstated on 6 September, 1776, and his daughter Eugénie was born the following year, to his mistress Marie-Thérèse de Willermaulaz, whom he would marry almost a decade later. In July of 1778, also, Beaumarchais had the satisfaction of finally winning his case against the Comte de la Blache, over the Pâris-Duverney affair. In the same year, the great Voltaire made a much-heralded return to Paris from exile, and died there on 25 May. Although at least half of Voltaire's books had been banned in France, there was a rising clamour for publication of his complete works, and indeed an offer to do so had already come from Catherine the Great. Beaumarchais, indignant at the very idea that Voltaire might be first published in Russia, promptly created his own publishing company, expressly for the purpose, and since the printing couldn't safely be done in France, rented premises in

Kehl, Germany. Several fonts of Baskerville type, the very
best available, were imported from England, three paper-
mills were bought, and the process got under way in
1783. Not until 1790, in a radically changed world, was
Beaumarchais' edition of Voltaire published in full, by
which time he had incurred a huge financial loss.

Meanwhile, Beaumarchais had at last completed *The
Marriage of Figaro*, an outline of which had appeared as
early as 1775, in the author's preface to *The Barber of
Seville*. The play was given a public reading at the
Comédie Française on 29 September, 1781, when Louis
XVI reportedly took exception to its subversive content,
and banned it forthwith. Thus began a lengthy process of
revisions, private readings, submissions to various censors
– eventually six in total – and as Beaumarchais himself
declared, *The Marriage of Figaro* proved infinitely more
difficult to stage than to write. Interest in the new work
ran high, however, not least at Court, where Marie-
Antoinette and the King's brother, the Comte d'Artois,
pleaded Beaumarchais' cause, and Louis was finally
compelled to give way. *The Marriage of Figaro* was
premièred on 27 April, 1784, and ran uninterrupted at
the Comédie Française for the next eight months, an
unheard-of phenomenon.

Despite its success, or perhaps because of it, Beaumarchais
continued to be attacked in the press, and foolishly responded
by complaining about the 'lions and tigers' he had been
forced to wrestle with, to get the play staged. Louis XVI
chose to interpret this as a personal slight, and promptly
had Beaumarchais imprisoned in the St Lazare reformatory
for juvenile delinquents – humiliating for the writer, now
aged 52, but also damaging for the King, shown up in a

very public act of tyranny. Amicable relations were soon restored, however, and Beaumarchais was even invited to a performance of *The Barber of Seville*, on 19 August, 1785, at the Petit Trianon in the Palace of Versailles, with Marie-Antoinette and the Comte d'Artois playing Rosine and Figaro.

Beaumarchais' characters, meanwhile, who had already appeared in an English version at the Theatre Royal, Covent Garden, were about to move onto an even more exalted plane. Although the stage play was banned in Austria, Mozart and Da Ponte's operatic version of *The Marriage of Figaro* was premièred at the Vienna Burgtheater on 1 May, 1786. Curiously, Beaumarchais had to wait until May 1793 to hear the work which was to usurp his own fame, during a brief return to Paris at the height of the Terror, when he reportedly found Mozart's music tiresome. In Beaumarchais' defence, it must be said that he was by then almost totally deaf.

Beaumarchais' own attempt at writing an opera, *Tarare*, set to music specially commissioned from Mozart's rival Salieri, was in fact a modest success, staged in Paris in the summer of 1787, and its overtly political theme, that of tyranny overthrown, would guarantee continued interest in the piece in the years following the Revolution. Applying hindsight, Beaumarchais is often credited with both having foreseen the events of 1789, and helping to bring them about. How far the former, at any rate, is distant from the truth, may be estimated by the fact that two years earlier, in 1787, he bought some land in a quiet district of Paris near the Faubourg St Antoine, and began building the most extravagant house and garden imaginable – four gates, two hundred windows, central heating, imported

Italian marble; at a cost of over two million francs, the project almost ruined him, and in the harsh climate of the Revolution years, Beaumarchais' folly, as it was described, came near to costing him his life. Ironically, when Beaumarchais first surveyed his plot of land, virtually the only other building he could see was the Bastille!

Even before the storming of the Bastille on the 14th of July, 1789, the Paris mob had taken to looting and burning, and Beaumarchais only managed to save his own mansion by volunteering to supervise the demolition of the hated prison, though his property became a prime target for periodic searches, at first for a rumoured grain hoard, later for weapons. At the beginning of 1792, with France now at war, Beaumarchais was approached by an arms dealer, offering to supply 60,000 rifles, from a store in Holland. His American experience made him the obvious intermediary, and Beaumarchais was duly authorised by the revolutionary government to negotiate the purchase. This failed to prevent his arrest and confinement, however, in August of that year, and his release from the notorious Abbaye prison was only secured by the intercession of a former mistress, two days before the entire prison population was massacred, in a fresh outbreak of mob fury.

In Holland, Beaumarchais found his efforts to obtain the rifles obstructed at every turn – not least by the chaotic political situation in France itself, where at one stage, some fifteen different ministers of war were appointed and removed in less than six months. Without a doubt, it was only Beaumarchais' absence from Paris, during the worst years of the Terror, that saved his life, and even though he was abroad on official business, he was nonetheless declared a proscribed émigré. In July 1794, his property was confiscated, and his wife and sisters arrested and condemned to death. Ironically, while Beaumarchais' family was saved by the fall of Robespierre, his old enemy Goëzman was guillotined at this time.

Beaumarchais meanwhile spent a miserable two years in exile in Hamburg, shunned by the genuine émigrés, who knew him to be an agent of the revolutionary government. When he was finally able to return home, in July 1796, he had to re-marry his wife Marie-Thérèse, who had been compelled to divorce him to save her own life. Beaumarchais spent his last years trying to rebuild his shattered fortunes, while his numerous debtors, great and small, waited for him to pass on. On 18 May, 1799, he finally obliged them, dying of an apoplexy at his Paris mansion, thus ending what must surely rank among the most colourful and eventful lives of the eighteenth century.

The Marriage of Figaro: **What Happens in the Play**

The Marriage of Figaro is a sequel to the events depicted in *The Barber of Seville*, in which the resourceful Figaro outwits a certain Dr Bartholo, and secures the beautiful Rosine, Bartholo's ward and unwilling intended bride, for his master Count Almaviva, by an audacious intrigue involving bribery, numerous ingenious disguises, and sheer effrontery. All the principals – Bartholo, his go-between Bazile, Almaviva, Rosine, and of course Figaro, reappear in the later play, but the passage of time has somewhat changed their relationships. The Count has married his Rosine, the first bloom of romance has faded, and he is now chafing at his humdrum domestic existence. Figaro, now major-domo at the Castle of Aguas-Frescas, is engaged to marry Suzanne, the Countess's maid, with the Count's enthusiastic approval. The Count has designs on Suzanne himself, however, and fancies that a handsome dowry will tempt her to grant him the infamous *droit de seigneur*, i.e., the feudal lord's ancient right to bed his female servants before their wedding, although he has already abolished it throughout his estates. The Count's intermediary in this dishonorable cause is incidentally that same Bazile, now music-master at the Castle, who had acted in a similar capacity for Dr Bartholo in Seville. A further potential blight on Figaro's happiness is the presence of one Marceline, a waiting-woman from whom he has borrowed a large sum of money against a promise of marriage, should he default on repayment. Among a number of new characters, however, the most important is Chérubin, the Countess's lovestruck young page, who enters the lists as a possible rival to the Count for his own wife's affections.

The play opens with Figaro and Suzanne inspecting a room which the Count has gifted them as their nuptial suite, convenient for his own darker purposes. Figaro is naively pleased, but when Suzanne reveals how the Count is employing Bazile to put her virtue under siege, Figaro resolves to trap his master in an intrigue. Dr Bartholo, Figaro's former adversary from Seville, then enters with the unfortunate Marceline, who, it appears, had also had a promise of marriage from the Doctor, many years before. She begs him to help her win Figaro by frustrating the Count's designs on Suzanne, so that he will avenge himself by forcing Figaro to marry Marceline. Suzanne and Marceline then meet in a brief exchange of insults, masquerading as compliments, fuelled by their jealousy over Figaro. Next, Suzanne is approached by Chérubin, distraught because the Count intends to dismiss him over an indiscretion with the gardener's daughter, Fanchette. Chérubin, who is basically in love with love, professes himself heartbroken at the prospect of never again seeing his adored mistress, and when Suzanne produces one of the Countess's ribbons, he snatches it from her and the pair embark on a comic chase. At this point, the Count unexpectedly enters, and the terrified Chérubin hides behind an armchair.

Believing himself alone with Suzanne, the Count proceeds to make advances to her, which she vigorously repels, and when they in turn are suddenly interrupted by the entry of Bazile, looking for Figaro, the Count also hides behind the armchair, while Chérubin manages to find a new hiding-place in the nick of time. Bazile again pleads his master's cause with Suzanne, and accuses her of flirting with Chérubin, who has composed a love-song for some mysterious lady. If it isn't Suzanne, claims Bazile, then it must be the Countess, as indeed the kitchen gossip would have it. Hearing this, the Count leaps up from behind the armchair and declares that Chérubin is to be instantly dismissed. And when he discovers Chérubin also concealed in Suzanne's room, he accuses her of conducting a clandestine affair with the young page, in a show of sanctimonious indignation at her betrayal of his good friend Figaro.

A deputation of Castle servants and estate workers arrives in festive mood, led by Figaro, who cunningly delivers a speech in praise of the Count's progressive outlook, in having abolished the barbarous *droit de seigneur*. Effectively cornered, the Count is forced to join in the general goodwill. The Countess then persuades him to moderate

Chérubin's punishment and award the errant page a commission in his regiment, on condition that he leave to take up his post immediately. Figaro, however, advises Chérubin to stay, but keep out of sight, at least until the wedding festivities are over.

At the beginning of Act II, Suzanne tells the Countess of the incident with the ribbon, and Chérubin's infatuation with her. The Countess is far from amused, however, to learn of the Count's attempt to seduce Suzanne, and when Figaro joins them, they resolve to frustrate his plans with an intrigue of their own. In order to make the Count jealous, Figaro has already sent him a letter, through Bazile, warning him that a secret admirer would be in pursuit of the Countess at the ball. To ensnare the Count further, Figaro proposes to disguise Chérubin as Suzanne, and arrange a clandestine rendezvous for the pair. While the Countess is helping Chérubin into one of her dresses, however, the Count unexpectedly arrives, to be confronted by a locked door, and obvious sounds of panic within. The Countess locks Chérubin into Suzanne's boudoir, before admitting the Count, but his suspicions are aroused, and he threatens to break open the door, forcing the Countess to accompany him while he fetches the necessary tools. In their absence, Chérubin unlocks the door, and Suzanne takes his place, while he escapes out of the window.

Unaware of this, the Countess tearfully confesses all to the Count on their return and is as astonished as he, when the boudoir door is opened to disclose not Chérubin, but Suzanne! Mutual recriminations follow, but it is the Count who is compelled to beg forgiveness, and extend the same even to Figaro, when the latter is revealed as the true source of Bazile's mysterious warning note. At this point, the Count's gardener Antonio enters to complain about a man leaping out of the window onto his flower-beds. Figaro at first accuses Antonio of being drunk, then declares himself to be the culprit, having been concealed in Suzanne's room, and alarmed by the Count's threats. However, Antonio is in possession of a paper dropped by the fugitive, and the Count challenges Figaro to describe its contents. Luckily, the Countess is able to pass a message to him that it is in fact Chérubin's commission, and the danger is averted.

Figaro is still waiting for the Count to give formal consent for his wedding, and a serious obstacle now presents itself in the shape of Marceline, who demands that her case against Figaro be tried that very day, a request which the Count is only too pleased to grant. The Countess, meanwhile, in a last effort to bring her husband to heel, persuades Suzanne to arrange a rendezvous with him, which she herself will keep, disguised as Suzanne.

At the beginning of Act III, the Count attempts to discover how much Figaro knows about his designs upon Suzanne, and they discuss the Count's proposal to employ Figaro as his diplomatic courier in England – which will allow the Count ready access to Figaro's wife, during his necessary absences. Later, when the Count is alone, Suzanne enters to set in motion the first stage of the Countess's own scheme, unknown to Figaro, by agreeing to meet the Count in secret that evening. Suzanne is exultant, and tells Figaro he need no longer worry about Marceline, their case is as good as won. Unfortunately, the Count overhears them and resolves to place a further obstruction in their path, by encouraging Antonio, who happens to be Suzanne's uncle, and who despises Figaro, to refuse his niece permission to marry.

The main body of Act III is taken up with the trial, in which the examining magistrate, one Brid'oisin, is exposed as a logic-chopping fool, and carries the burden of Beaumarchais' satire against the corrupt and inefficient French judiciary at whose hands he had suffered so much. Predictably, Figaro loses his case, and is ordered to repay his debt to Marceline there and then, or else marry her. However, in a bizarre twist, it is discovered that Figaro is in fact Marceline's long-lost son, the product of her union, many years earlier, with Dr Bartholo. From embittered rival for Figaro's affections, Marceline is transformed into doting mother, and Antonio's objection to Figaro as a son-in-law is incidentally removed.

Act IV begins with the happy couple declaring their love, but Suzanne is still secretly involved in the Countess's plot to ensnare the Count, and writes a letter arranging to meet him that night in the garden. The preliminaries to Figaro's wedding can now begin, and the village girls enter in festive attire. Among them, however, is Chérubin, in disguise, and when he is exposed by Antonio, the Count threatens to punish him severely. At this point, the maid Fanchette comes to Chérubin's rescue, by naively confessing the Count's own indiscretions with her, and the Count is forced to back down. Later that evening, Suzanne's compromising letter is passed to him, with instructions to return the pin with which it is sealed, as a sign that he has understood the message. The Count gives the pin to Fanchette, however, who unwittingly reveals all to Figaro, convincing the latter that his future wife is about to betray him.

Suzanne's pretended assignation with the Count is scheduled to take place in a chestnut grove, and Act V begins with Figaro concealed there in the darkness, lamenting his unhappy fate and the deceit of women. In the course of a long soliloquy, he also gloomily reviews his past life, much of which so nearly recalls the experience of Beaumarchais himself as to be autobiographical. Confident that both the Count and his faithless bride-to-be are about to be exposed, Figaro has invited the entire company to witness the scandal, and the scene is set for an intricate and fast-moving farce. Suzanne and the Countess are of course present, dressed in each other's clothes; so also is Chérubin, who contrives to get mixed up in the action, to the extent of kissing the Count by mistake for the Countess, and avoiding the slap the Count aims at him, which lands on Figaro instead.

Darkness, and the various disguises, ensure a rich vein of misunderstanding. The Count pays court to Suzanne, as he imagines her to be, while in reality trying to explain his marital discontent to its supposed source, the Countess herself. Next Suzanne, disguised as the Countess, makes a similar approach to Figaro; the latter recognizes her voice, however, and mischievously pretends to be in love with the 'Countess', which earns him another slap. Explanations are exchanged, and the pair then stage a love-scene for the Count's benefit – Suzanne is of course still dressed as the Countess, and the Count is persuaded to believe that his wife is having an affair with Figaro. Outraged, he denounces her in front of the entire company, refusing to hear any plea on her behalf. In a brilliant *coup de théâtre*, the real Countess then emerges from the summer-house, and joins the kneeling supplicants. The Count is humiliated, and compelled to beg the Countess for forgiveness, which she graciously grants. Finally, the company perform a 'vaudeville', in which each of the principals recounts in song their version of events.

Beaumarchais the Dramatist

Beaumarchais' fame as a dramatist nowadays rests on the two plays of his Figaro trilogy, *The Barber of Seville* (1775) and *The Marriage of Figaro* (1784), and that chiefly due to their after-life in opera, at the hands of Rossini and Mozart. The third Figaro play, *The Guilty Mother* (1792), is relatively little known, and the same is true of Beaumarchais' first essays in dramatic form, though they are historically important in the development of theatrical realism.

Beaumarchais in fact began writing for performance in the 1760's with a series of 'Parades', racy satirical sketches which he created for the private theatre of Charles d'Etiolles, the wealthy former husband of Mme de Pompadour. These are already distinguished by that demotic vigour of expression and wordplay which characterise his mature work, but his serious ambition as a dramatist derives from the theory and practice of Denis Diderot (1713-1784), and the latter's campaign to reform the French theatre. As late as 1759, the Comédie Française was still selling seats on the stage, which made any attempt at naturalism virtually impossible. In Diderot's view, moreover, French theatre was severely restricted by its dominant genres, in particular the classical tragedy, inherited from Corneille and Racine, which still rigidly observed the unities of time, place and action, and more damagingly, a classical decorum of speech, favouring generalised abstraction, at the expense of concreteness, and enlivening detail.

Comedy, over which hung the shadow of Molière, was likewise perceived to be in a rut, peopled with largely stereotyped personifications of character traits, going through the motions in mechanistic plots. Diderot's argument, the theory of which was more convincing than his own practice, was that the theatre should concern itself with the lives of ordinary middle-class people, not mythical kings and heroes. In this new type of drama, the *drame bourgeois*, plays should be in prose, not verse, and the dialogue straightforward and natural, while the shock tactic *coup de théâtre* should give way to what Diderot called the *tableau*, the meaningful stage grouping of relationships. Diderot's *Le Fils naturel* and *Le Père de famille*, written to illustrate these theories, and published in the late 1750's, exercised a strong influence on Beaumarchais' first serious plays, *Eugénie* (1767), and *The Two Friends* (1770).

Though he had begun work on *Eugénie* as early as 1759, Beaumarchais draws on his own experience in the Clavijo affair of 1764, since the plot centres on the plight of a virtuous young woman who has been tricked into a mock marriage, and the determination of the heroine's brother to either avenge her, or force her aristocratic betrayer to do the decent thing, recalling Beaumarchais' efforts on behalf of his sister Lisette in Madrid. Typically, however, it also attacks the privileges of the nobility, and Beaumarchais had to appease the censor by transporting his characters from their original French setting, in Brittany, to England. After an unhappy première at the Comédie Française, on 29 January, 1767, *Eugénie* went on to enjoy considerable success, and was even performed in an English version, titled *The School for Rakes*, by Garrick at Drury Lane in London.

Beaumarchais' second play in the *drame bourgeois* idiom, *The Two Friends, or The Merchant of Lyon*, conforms more closely to Diderot's criteria, since the dramatic connection between the friends, a silk merchant and a tax collector, derives from their everyday occupations, which Beaumarchais describes in some detail, and the crisis is precipitated by an event well within the experience of the playwright's contemporaries. In brief, the silk merchant is about to go bankrupt, when he is rescued by a substantial loan from his tax-gatherer friend. Unfortunately, the latter has had to use tax monies already collected to do so, and a surprise visit from the authorities leaves him open to a charge of embezzlement. All ends happily, however, when the embezzler's honourable motives are revealed, and his superior even makes the silk merchant a personal loan, to re-establish his business. The plot is spiced up with a conventional love interest, but the complexities of high finance, on which the drama turns, failed to excite the audience at its Paris opening, at the Comédie Française on 13 January, 1770, and *The Two Friends* was taken off after a modest ten performances. Beaumarchais' commitment to Diderot's *genre sérieux* remained strong, nonetheless, and as well as returning to it for his final Figaro play, *The Guilty Mother* (1792), its influence on the more celebrated comedies is clear, in their lively demotic speech, and detailed texture.

Beaumarchais first intended *The Barber of Seville* as a comic opera, for the Comédie Italienne, and when that was rejected, re-wrote it as a five-act play, to be premièred at

the Comédie Française on 12 February, 1774.
Unfortunately, the infamous Goëzman affair was at its
height, and the scandal caused by the publication of
Beaumarchais' fourth *Mémoire* made it too much of a risk
for the theatre. The production was suspended for a year,
and *The Barber of Seville* was eventually staged on 23
February, 1775. Beaumarchais was unable to resist settling
a few scores in the play, and the audience made their
displeasure vocal. Not for the first time, however, the
author revised his text, cutting out a full act, and the new
version was triumphantly received two days later. By
comparison with its sequel, *The Barber of Seville* is relatively
straightforward, and its theme, that of an old man vainly
attempting to beat off younger and more virile
competition for his intended bride, has a pedigree dating
back to antiquity, including a number of French
exemplars, notably Molière's *École des femmes*.

The character of the resourceful valet, who helps his master
to his young bride, outwitting her guardian, is also familiar,
not least from the stock figures of the *commedia dell'arte*, which
had been such an influence on Molière. Beaumarchais'
Figaro, however, is unique in having a life beyond his plot
function, which enriches all his relationships, with the
Count, for example, but also his elderly adversary, Dr
Bartholo. Scholars have noted that in the French of
Beaumarchais' day, *fils Caron* ('Caron the son') would have
been pronounced 'fi Caron', suggesting the close affinity
between Beaumarchais and his creation, and it is
undoubtedly that element of identification which makes
Figaro so complex and rounded a character. Beaumarchais
had already hinted at a sequel, in a preface to *The Barber
of Seville*, and later confessed to having warned the Prince

de Conti, who urged him to write it, that an older Figaro would assuredly be wiser, and even more critical of society, than his original exuberant barber-valet. That was indeed the case, when he came to write his masterpiece, *The Marriage of Figaro*, which was given its first public reading at the Comédie Française on 29 September, 1781.

Figaro three years older is certainly wiser, even embittered at times, and Beaumarchais' own experience in the interim may credibly be argued to have played a part in that. The prime target of Figaro's scheming is no longer the conventional old fool, but his aristocratic master, a man more or less his own age, whose morally repugnant designs on Figaro's fiancée are only conceivable in a society in which power and privilege can be abused without hindrance. While Beaumarchais' hero has lost none of that dazzling wit, which prompted one contemporary critic to describe him as 'a talking machine', *The Marriage of Figaro* is less of a 'comedy of intrigue' than its predecessor, and more an exploration of themes, some of them decidedly sombre. Count Almaviva, still charming and personable, is now the bored husband, well on the way to becoming a heartless womaniser, while his wife, the vivacious Rosine of *The Barber of Seville*, has changed almost beyond recognition – infinitely more knowing, and disillusioned. However, the theme of betrayal and soured relationships is interwoven throughout with that of class conflict, voiced not only by Figaro, but even on occasion by Suzanne, and it gives Beaumarchais' comedy very sharp teeth indeed.

Although set in Spain to placate the censor, *The Marriage of Figaro* was originally set in France, and it is his own society which is the target of Beaumarchais' criticism, notably in Figaro's long monologue in Act V, where he strikes at the very root of privilege, the accident of birth which makes one man grotesquely powerful, and another a slave, regardless of their merits. Through Figaro, Beaumarchais also attacks the absurdity of censorship, which his own experience well illustrates, and given his sufferings at the hands of the French judicial system, the satire of the court proceedings in Act III is if anything mild, even though he names his chief legal buffoon Don *Gusman* Brid'oisin, an obvious jibe at his enemy Goëzman. Where Molière, for example, denied satirising real persons, Beaumarchais made little effort to disguise his targets, and the arch-villain of his later years, a professional slanderer by the name of Bergasse, appears in *The Guilty Mother* as the malignant hypocrite Bégearss.

Settling scores, however entertainingly, would not be sufficient to make *The Marriage of Figaro* the great comedy of ideas which it undoubtedly is. Figaro's Act V soliloquy goes on to explore much deeper waters, the riddle of his own identity, and that of man in general. In that respect, it is significant that the master-intriguer of *The Barber of Seville*, pulling all the strings, seems to have lost his sure touch in the later play, and frequently takes a back seat to Suzanne, or the Countess, or indeed Marceline, whose Act III revelation that Figaro is her long-lost son abruptly terminates a major strand of plot, and incidentally recreates her as a character. Marceline is also the spokesperson for Beaumarchais' advanced views on the rights of women, in a fierce tirade against double standards, which the Comédie Française actors refused to perform, partly because it sits so uneasily in the comic mainstream.

Structurally, in fact, *The Marriage of Figaro* is awkward, or at least unconventional – the comedy delivers its routine

happy ending in Act IV, with the marriage of Figaro and
Suzanne, and Marceline and Bartholo, then restarts under
the Countess's direction, so to speak, as she schemes to
repair her own marriage, in the course of a brilliant farce
sequence which would do credit to Feydeau. However,
that is also to the credit of Beaumarchais' wayward
genius, and although our attention is often diverted, by
one sub-plot or another, the principal conflict, that
between Figaro and Count Almaviva, is kept in focus
throughout, until all is finally revealed, and resolved, in
the illuminating darkness of Act V.

That Beaumarchais identifies with Figaro is undeniable,
but the connection is more subtle than in *The Barber of
Seville*, and it is worth reiterating how much less secure is
Figaro's grip on events, where Chérubin, for example,
seems to function as a sort of 'loose cannon', introducing
an element of the unpredictable at several key moments in
the play. Like Marceline, who never appears in *The Barber
of Seville*, Chérubin is a new character, and his impact on
the play, part-catalyst, part-irritant, might almost be
summed up in the farcical incident in Act V, where he
manages to get himself in the way, and receives the kiss
from the Count, intended for Suzanne – the fact that
Figaro himself then receives the blow intended for
Chérubin underscores the point.

Chérubin reappears, but only by report, in the third play
of the trilogy, *The Guilty Mother* (1792) in which we revisit
the characters some twenty years later, and a world away
from the sparkling cut-and-thrust of its precursors. The
Almaviva household has been relocated from Spain to
post-Revolutionary Paris, and the plot revolves around the
existence, unknown to each other, of the Count and

Countess's illegitimate son and daughter, who are incidentally in love. Rosine's son is the product of an affair with Chérubin, who has died in battle many years previously. Figaro ultimately rights all wrongs, but the prime mover of the action is Bégearss, the Count's villainous adviser, and in its moral earnestness, the play more closely resembles the Diderot-influenced dramas of Beaumarchais' early years. It is altogether a darker piece, in keeping with the times, and it brings to an end Beaumarchais' career in the theatre. Beaumarchais was very soon forced to quit France, but he would scarcely have thrived in the kind of atmosphere created by the Convention decree of the following year, which ruled that certain politically approved plays were to be staged each week by law, and also threatened dire punishment for anyone producing plays which might corrupt the public – an early foretaste of cultural policy in Stalin's Russia.

By Beaumarchais' own admission, the loose structure of *The Marriage of Figaro* is an inevitable result of his intention to make the play a vehicle for social criticism, and there is no denying its contribution to the current of ideas which shaped the modern world. Nonetheless, to see Beaumarchais as the harbinger of red revolution is to apply the wisdom of hindsight too freely, and he remained a loyal servant of the *ancien régime* almost to the end – a gradualist reformer, and French patriot, rather than a radical ideologue. In truth, although his writings, dramatic and other, embody the most stinging critique of his society, they express only what was already being said on the streets of Paris. At the furthest extreme from the political, however, it is the uniquely personal, idiosyncratic character of that expression which has made his Figaro the universal type of the common man, rising in the world on his merits, in heroic defiance of entrenched power.

Beaumarchais and Opera

Although Beaumarchais strongly believed in the primacy of the word over music, it is worth recalling that *The Barber of Seville* first took shape as an *opera buffa*, unsuccessfully submitted to the popular Comédie Italienne. However, following its triumphant success as a play, Giovanni Paisiello, court composer to Catherine the Great, turned it into a two-act opera, which was premièred in St Petersburg on 15 September, 1782. Paisiello's opera was performed all over Europe, including Vienna, where Mozart undoubtedly heard it before making his own attempt on Beaumarchais, with *The Marriage of Figaro*. Lorenzo da Ponte, Mozart's librettist, had to work in secret, since the play was banned in Vienna, but much of its subversive content was jettisoned in the adaptation – Figaro's Act V monologue, for example, and the court-room satire – and the Emperor eventually approved the work for performance. Premièred on 1 May, 1786 at the Burgtheater, *Le Nozze di Figaro* enjoyed considerable success, though it was not performed in Paris until the spring of 1793, when Beaumarchais rather unwisely insisted on inserting passages of his original text into the opera, which suffered as a consequence.

Possibly stimulated by news of Mozart's venture, Beaumarchais created a new opera of his own, for which he invited Salieri to supply the music, and even lodged the composer in his Paris house. *Tarare*, an exotic narrative celebrating the struggle of the common man against tyranny, was premièred on 8 June, 1787, and proved especially popular during the Revolution years, when it was regularly revised in line with the political requirements of the day.

The other great Beaumarchais opera, Rossini's *Barber of Seville*, was written long after the playwright's death, although Paisiello was still alive at the time of its première, at the Teatro Argentina in Rome, on 20 February, 1816, so that Rossini was forced to change the title, out of respect for his distinguished predecessor. Paisiello died soon after, however, and Rossini's *Barber of Seville*, based on a libretto by Sterbini, went on to join Mozart's *Marriage of Figaro* in the classic repertoire. The first London performance of Rossini's opera was given at the Haymarket Theatre and Covent Garden, in 1818, surprisingly just a few years after the London première of *The Marriage of Figaro*, which took place at the Haymarket in 1812.

To complete the set, the third play of the Figaro trilogy, *The Guilty Mother*, has also entered the operatic repertoire in more recent times, in versions by Milhaud (1966), and Corigliano (1991), but if he had done nothing more than furnish Mozart and Rossini with the canvases on which to create their master-works, Beaumarchais would have earned the admiration of opera-goers everywhere. Unfortunately, in the English-speaking world at least, the great operas have tended to distract attention from Beaumarchais' original genius as a dramatist. In the theatre of his own day, tragedy was the dominant mode, while comedy had become increasingly formulaic. Beaumarchais re-acquainted the stage not only with the language of the streets, but also a vital comic energy that had been diminishing since Molière. Finally, the innovative *drames bourgeois* of his early years, though now largely forgotten, play an important role in the development of realism in the European theatre.

The Comédie Française

The world's oldest permanent national theatre, the Comédie Française, was established in 1680 following a series of mergers, as one of three official theatres in Paris, the others being the Opéra and the Comédie Italienne. Louis XIV granted the Comédie Française the exclusive right to perform plays in French, a monopoly which lasted until the Revolution, when the company split into two factions, the more conservative of which barely managed to escape the guillotine. Removed to its present site, in a former opera house in the Rue de Richelieu in 1799, the Comédie Française was reconstituted by the Emperor Napoleon, in a decree signed in Moscow in October1812, a few days before his ignominious retreat. In the course of its history, the Comédie Française has witnessed some momentous events, and itself undergone radical change, but even today its organisation would be familiar to Molière, with its rigid hierarchy of probationers, and full members, the *sociétaires*, actor-shareholders, who determine the company's artistic policy, take a share of the profits, and retire on pension after twenty years' service.

Beaumarchais' involvement with the Comédie Française came at a particularly interesting phase of its physical development. Many of the older French theatres had been designed originally as indoor tennis courts, and it was not until 1782 that the company was able to move into a purpose-built theatre (the modern Odéon) in the Faubourg Saint-Germain, following a brief temporary sojourn in the Salle des Machines in the Tuileries. The theatre at the Tuileries, where Beaumarchais' *Barber of Seville* was premièred in 1775, was roundly disliked by the Comédie Française actors, but at least they no longer had to endure the presence of spectators on stage, a practice which the company was able to abandon in 1759, following a donation from a wealthy patron, to compensate for loss of earnings. Prior to that, as many as 200 spectators, over-dressed fops for the most part, might be seated on benches on the stage, or lounging in the wings, which made any sort of complex *mise-en-scène* impossible.

At its handsome new Odéon theatre the Comédie Française also installed seats in the *parterre*, or pit, which restricted audience movement, and taken along with important changes in lighting, significantly enhanced performance. Earlier in the century, the stage was lit by an overhead chandelier; by Beaumarchais' day, however, footlight and wing lighting had been intensified, and the stage could also be lit 'naturally', by candelabra and lamps. As a consequence of these innovations, scenic design became far more ambitious; the stage could be furnished to a much greater extent than before, and actors' movements blocked in much more detail. Beaumarchais' commitment to realism demanded no less, and it is on record that he devoted an exceptional thirty rehearsals to a production of *The Barber of Seville* in Brussels, in 1776.

Our modern concept of auditorium and stage as separate worlds had yet to develop, however, and there was a great deal of vocal interaction between actors and their clearly visible audience. Indeed, it was not uncommon for performers even to argue with the prompt, whose head and shoulders could be seen above the level of the footlights. The theatrical illusion was also not aided by the prevailing standards of on-stage decorum. One English visitor to the Comédie Française in this period was greatly impressed by the performance of the actresses, but rather less by their habit of hawking and spitting when the need arose. Theatre-going was an altogether more boisterous experience in Beaumarchais' day, and in common with other companies, the Comédie Française routinely passed out tickets to paid supporters, the notorious *claque*, with precise instructions on when to applaud. Even without their artificial enthusiasm, however, *The Marriage of Figaro* ran for over five hours at its première in 1784, with the audience wildly cheering every other line.

Over the three centuries of its existence, the Comédie Française has regularly expanded and modernised its repertoire, but it is still dominated by the great names of its classical tradition. Beaumarchais' plays have been largely eclipsed in England by the Mozart and Rossini operas, though there have been notable productions, including Jonathan Miller's *Marriage of Figaro*, at the National Theatre in 1970, and a BBC Radio 3 airing of the Figaro trilogy in 1984, with Dorothy Tutin as Rosine. In France, however, the Comédie Française has kept faith with the playwright, and although productions of his work fall far short of Molière's record (the runaway winner, with some thirty thousand) Beaumarchais' score of over three thousand separate stagings in the company's history, is evidence of his secure place in the repertoire.

For Further Reading

The standard edition of Beaumarchais' works in French is *Oeuvres*, edited by P. Larthomas for Gallimard (Bibliothèque de la Pléiade), Paris, 1988. Among translations, John Wells' version of the Figaro trilogy, published by J M Dent, 1997, includes a valuable appendix section, of Beaumarchais' own prefaces to the plays. Since so much of his writing is drawn directly from the events of his extraordinary life, biography is a particularly useful entry-point to the plays, though one should beware of identifying Beaumarchais too closely with the character of Figaro, which tends to devalue his creative genius. This is to some extent the case with Frédéric Grendel's *Beaumarchais ou la Calomnie*, Flammarion, Paris 1973, translated by Roger Greaves as *Beaumarchais: The Man Who Was Figaro*, Macdonald and Jane's, 1977, which although an entertaining read, occasionally treats the plays as an extension of the biography. Despite its title, Cynthia Cox's *The Real Figaro*, Longmans, 1962, is a more straightforward account of Beaumarchais' life, and there are good studies of the plays by Joseph Sungolowsky, in *Beaumarchais*, in the Twayne's World Authors Series, Twayne Publishers, Inc., New York, 1974, and of *The Marriage of Figaro* specifically, in Anthony R Pugh's *Beaumarchais: Le Mariage de Figaro*, Macmillan, 1968. William D Howarth's excellent *Beaumarchais and the Theatre*, Routledge, 1995, gives a scholarly account of French theatre in the 17th and 18th centuries, as background to a detailed analysis of Beaumarchais' dramatic output. Finally, the same author's *French Theatre in the Neo-Classical Era*, Cambridge University Press, 1997, is a fascinating anthology of original documents on every aspect of theatre life in the period.

Beaumarchais: Key Dates

1732   Born Pierre-Augustin de Caron, in Paris, 24 January, only surviving son among five daughters. Father a master clockmaker.

1745   Enters his father's trade as apprentice.

1753   Invents a regulatory device for clocks, his invention stolen by the royal clockmaker, M. Lepaute.

1754   Beaumarchais successfully appeals to the Académie des Sciences, making his name at Court, which enables him to purchase a sinecure, *Contrôleur de la Bouche du Roi*.

1756   Marries the widow of his predecessor in that office, assumes the name Beaumarchais from one of her properties.

1757   Wife dies, Beaumarchais involved in protracted litigation over claims on her estate.

1759   Beaumarchais undertakes to teach the harp to the King's daughters.

1760   Makes the acquaintance of the financier Pâris-Duverney, who takes charge of Beaumarchais' business affairs.

1761   Purchases the office of *Sécretaire du Roi*, which confers noble rank.

1763   Appointed to the post of *Lieutenant-Général des Chasses*, responsible for enforcing the game laws in the royal domain.

1764:   Travels to Spain, to vindicate his sister's honour in a breach of promise case. The 'Clavijo affair' as it is known, becomes the talk of Europe, and the subject of a play by Goethe (*Clavigo*,1774).

1767   Première of his first play, *Eugénie*, at the Comédie Française, 29 January.

1768   Marries wealthy widow, Geneviève Madeleine Wattbled, 11 April. Birth of son, Pierre-Augustin Eugène, 14 December.

1770   Première of second play, *The Two Friends* (*Les Deux Amis, ou le Négociant de Lyon*, 13 January; a failure, withdrawn after twelve performances. Death of Pâris-Duverney, 17 July; begins protracted legal battle with his heir, the Comte de la Blache. Death of second wife, 20 November.

1772   Wins case against La Blache, who lodges appeal with so-called 'Maupeou' Parlement. Death of son Eugène, 17 October.

1773   3 January, rehearsals of *The Barber of Seville* (*Le Barbier de Séville*) begun at the Comédie Française. 11 February, violent altercation with Duc de Chaulnes, both men briefly imprisoned. *The Barber of Seville* suspended. 1 April, M. Goëzman appointed to examine the La Blache case. Beaumarchais accused of bribery, involving Mme. Goëzman. 1 September, Beaumarchais publishes first of several *Mémoires* on the Goëzman affair, arouses public opinion against corrupt Parlement.

1774   26 February, judgement pronounced against both Beaumarchais and Mme. Goëzman, deprived of their civil rights. March-April, sent on secret mission to England, to suppress scandalous pamphlet on Madame Du Barry; 10 May, death of Louis XV; June-October, sent abroad on second secret mission, to suppress libellous pamphlet on the new Queen, Marie-Antoinette.

1775   23 February, première of *The Barber of Seville* in five acts, at the Comédie Française – initially a failure, reduced to four acts, re-staged three days later, a resounding success.

1776   10 June, Beaumarchais enlists government support for the insurgent American colonists against England. Granted a personal loan of two million livres, he equips a fleet to transport weapons and supplies to the colonists, guaranteeing their success in the campaign of 1777. 6 September, Beaumarchais' civil rights reinstated.

1777   Birth of daughter, Eugénie. Beaumarchais will marry her mother, Marie-Thérèse de Willermaulaz in 1786.

1778   13 March, France recognises the United States. Congress promises to repay Beaumarchais the massive debt he has incurred on their behalf. Not until 1835, long after his death, was this commitment honoured, and then only in part.

1779   Beaumarchais undertakes to publish the complete works of Voltaire, banned in France, sets up publishing house in Kehl (Germany) the following year.

1781   29 September, public reading of *The Marriage of Figaro* (*Le Mariage de Figaro*) at the Comédie Française. Louis XVI forbids its representation; the play begins a lengthy process of successive censorships.

1783   First volumes of the Kehl edition of Voltaire appear, a financial disaster for Beaumarchais.

1784   27 April, after passing through six different censorships, *The Marriage of Figaro* is premièred at the Comédie Française, a spectacular triumph.

1785   8 – 13 March, following an indiscreet criticism of their Majesties, in connection with the censorship, Beaumarchais is briefly confined in a prison for juvenile delinquents. 19 August, *The Barber of Seville* is performed at the Petit Trianon, with Marie-Antoinette playing Rosine.

1786   1 May, first performance of Mozart's *Le Nozze di Figaro* at the Vienna Burgtheater.

1789   14 July, fall of the Bastille. August, Beaumarchais elected a deputy of the Commune de Paris, charged with overseeing the demolition of the Bastille. A few weeks later, Beaumarchais is denounced and briefly expelled from the Assembly.

1792   26 June, première of *The Guilty Mother* (*La Mère coupable*) at the Théâtre du Marais. 11 August, Paris mob break into Beaumarchais' house, searching for concealed weapons. 23 August, Beaumarchais arrested. 2 – 6 September, massacres in Paris prisons, Beaumarchais released just in time. 22 September, leaves France with government commission to purchase rifles in Holland.

1793   21 January, execution of Louis XVI, the French Republic declares war on England and Holland. Beaumarchais returns to Paris, summoned to appear before the Committee of Public Safety. Pronounced innocent, Beaumarchais is again sent abroad on diplomatic business. 13 July, assassination of Marat, by Charlotte Corday. 16 October, execution of Marie-Antoinette.

1794   14 March, Beaumarchais is formally inscribed in the list of émigrés, despite his diplomatic mission. 10 June, beginning of the Terror. 4 July, Beaumarchais' family placed under arrest. 28 July, execution of Robespierre. 15 August, Beaumarchais' wife compelled to divorce him, as a proscribed émigré (they will remarry three years later).

1795   May-June, the 'White Terror', massacre of Jacobins at Lyon and Marseille.

1796   June, Beaumarchais' name finally removed from the list of émigrés; he returns to Paris the following month.

1799   18 May, dies of apoplexy.

THE MARRIAGE OF FIGARO

Characters

COUNT ALMAVIVA, *Chief magistrate of Andalusia.*
THE COUNTESS, *his wife.*
FIGARO, *his manservant and major-domo.*
SUZANNE, *the Countess's maid, and Figaro's fiancée.*
MARCELINE, *housekeeper.*
ANTONIO, *the castle gardener, Suzanne's uncle, and Fanchette's father.*
FANCHETTE, *Antonio's daughter.*
CHÉRUBIN, *the Count's page.*
BARTHOLO, *a doctor from Seville.*
BAZILE, *the Countess's music master.*
DON GUSMAN BRID'OISIN, *a local magistrate.*
DOUBLE-MAIN, *a clerk, Brid'oisin's secretary.*
GRIPE-SOLEIL, *a shepherd lad.*
PÉDRILLE, *the Count's huntsman.*
A Court Usher
A Young Shepherdess
Servants and Peasants.

The scene is the castle of Aguas-Frescas, about twenty miles from Seville.

3

ACT ONE

The stage represents a bedroom half-cleared of furniture; a high-backed chair in the middle of the room. FIGARO *is measuring the floor with a six-foot rule, while* SUZANNE *stands before a mirror, trying on a chaplet of orange-blossom, of the sort known as a 'bride's crown'.*

FIGARO. Nineteen feet by twenty-six.

SUZANNE. Look, Figaro – my little crown. Is it better like this, do you think?

FIGARO *(takes her hands in his)*. Absolutely perfect, my darling. Ah, that enchanting virginal wreath of flowers round a young girl's head, on her wedding day – in the eyes of her adoring bridegroom, what could be sweeter?

SUZANNE *(pulling away from him)*. What's that you're measuring, my love?

FIGARO. Well, my little Suzanne, I'm just looking to see if that fine bed which His Lordship is giving us will fit in here.

SUZANNE. In this room?

FIGARO. Yes, he's letting us have it.

SUZANNE. Well, I don't want it.

FIGARO. Why not?

SUZANNE. I just don't.

FIGARO. But why?

SUZANNE. I don't like it.

FIGARO. You might at least give a reason.

SUZANNE. What if I don't want to?

FIGARO. Honestly! Once they're certain they've got us!

SUZANNE. Giving a reason would be tantamount to
admitting I could be wrong. Are you my devoted slave or
not?

FIGARO. You've taken a dislike to the most comfortable
room in the castle, and it's in between the two
apartments, what's more. If Her Ladyship feels poorly
during the night, she'll ring from her side, and hey
presto! a couple of steps and you're in her room. If His
Lordship wants something, all he need do is give a little
tinkle, and *voilà!* – I'm with him in two shakes!

SUZANNE. Oh, very nice! But what about when he gives a
little tinkle in the morning, and sends you off on some
long, complicated errand? Then it'll be hey presto! a
couple of steps and he's at my door, and *voilà!* – in two
shakes . . .

FIGARO. What on earth do you mean?

SUZANNE. Listen to me, Figaro, and please keep calm.

FIGARO. What's all this about? Good God!

SUZANNE. It's about the fact that His Lordship, Count
Almaviva, has grown weary of chasing after the local
beauties, and feels like returning to his castle – not,
however, to his own wife, but yours. It's your wife he
has his eye on, do you understand? And putting us in this
room, he thinks, won't harm his chances. Anyway, that's
what Bazile, my esteemed singing teacher, who organises

His Lordship's pleasures for him, tells me every day while he's giving me my lesson.

FIGARO. Bazile! Well, my fine fellow, if ever a sound whipping, applied to a man's back, could give the marrow in his spine a good shake-up . . .

SUZANNE. My dear boy, did you honestly think this dowry His Lordship's giving me was in recognition of your merits?

FIGARO. I had done enough to hope so, yes.

SUZANNE. You know, clever people can be extremely foolish.

FIGARO. So they say.

SUZANNE. But they don't want to believe it.

FIGARO. Well, they're wrong.

SUZANNE. Anyway, you should be aware that he plans to use this room some time to get me on my own, and secretly obtain his ancient right from me – the *droit de seigneur* . . . And you know what that means.

FIGARO. I know this much – if His Lordship hadn't abolished that shameful law when he himself got married, I'd never have married you on his estate.

SUZANNE. Well, if he did abolish it, he's changed his mind. And he's now trying to buy it back in secret, from your fiancée.

FIGARO (*rubbing his forehead*). You know, I feel quite giddy from the shock, and there's something taking root . . .

SUZANNE. Don't rub it, then!

FIGARO. What's wrong?

SUZANNE. Well, if you get a little lump there, superstitious people will say . . .

FIGARO. You're laughing at me, you hussy! Oh, if only there were some way of catching this sly devil out, of drawing him into a trap, and pocketing his money!

SUZANNE. Intrigue and money – you're in your element now.

FIGARO. It's not shame that's holding me back.

SUZANNE. What, fear?

FIGARO. No, running risks is nothing, it's managing to get out of a dangerous situation, with some benefit. I mean, what could be easier than slipping into some fellow's house at night, taking advantage of his wife, and getting soundly thrashed for your pains? Couldn't be simpler, thousands of halfwitted rascals have done it. But . . . (*A bell is rung.*)

SUZANNE. That's Her Ladyship awake now. She specifically asked me to be the first person to speak to her on my wedding day.

FIGARO. What, is there something significant in that?

SUZANNE. Country people say it brings good luck to neglected wives. Anyway, dear Fi – Fi – Figaro, goodbye! Think about what I've said.

FIGARO. Give me a little kiss, to lift my spirits.

SUZANNE. What, kiss my lover today? Indeed I shan't! What will my husband say about that tomorrow? (FIGARO *kisses her.*) Well, really!

FIGARO. You have no idea how much I love you.

SUZANNE (*disengaging herself*). Honestly, you keep telling me that, from morning to night! When are you going to stop?

FIGARO (*archly*). Not until I can prove it to you from night to morning! (*The bell is rung again.*)

SUZANNE (*at a safe distance, blows him a kiss*). There's your kiss back, sir. I want nothing more from you now.

FIGARO (*runs after her*). Ah, but that's not the way you got it!

Exit SUZANNE.

FIGARO (*alone*). What a delightful girl! Always laughing, bubbling over, full of gaiety and wit, love and delight. Yet so good! . . . (*He walks briskly up and down, rubbing his hands.*) Well, dear lord and master, you want to make a fool of me, do you? I did wonder why, having put me in charge here, he was going to take me away with him on his embassy, and appoint me his letter-carrier. Yes, now I understand, sir – it's a triple promotion: you to ministerial envoy; me to hell-for-leather despatch-rider; and Suzanne to bit on the side, the ambassador's mistress – then it'll be – 'Off you go, Figaro!' And while I'm galloping in one direction, you'll be heading down another fine road with my beautiful girl! I'll be battling through the mud for the glory of your family, while you deign to have a hand in the increase of mine! A nice little tit-for-tat! Well, sir, you can go too far. To be doing both your master's job and your manservant's at the same time, representing the King, and myself, in foreign parts, so to speak, is just too much – it's a bit thick. And as for you, Bazile, you old lecher, I'll teach you a thing or two. By God, I'll . . . no, no, we'll have to put on a show, to set one against the other. Attend to your day's work, my dear Figaro! First, bring forward the time of your wedding, to make sure you're well and truly married. Get rid of that Marceline, who's so besotted with you; pocket the money and the gifts; put a spoke in His Lordship's little wheel of passion; give Bazile a good hiding, and then . . .

Breaks off as MARCELINE *and* BARTHOLO *enter.*

Aha! Here comes the stout doctor. We've a full hand now. Good day to you, dear doctor! Is it my wedding with Suzanne that brings you to the castle?

BARTHOLO (*disdainfully*). Huh! Not at all, my dear sir!

FIGARO. No, that would be too generous of you.

BARTHOLO. Indeed it would, and very foolish besides.

FIGARO. Since I had the misfortune to upset yours.

BARTHOLO. Have you anything else to say?

FIGARO. They're taking good care of your mule, I hope?

BARTHOLO (*angrily*). You raving lunatic! Leave us!

FIGARO. What, are you annoyed, doctor? People in your profession are so hard-hearted! No more pity for the poor animals – and that's a fact – than if they were men! Well, goodbye, Marceline – are you still planning to sue me? 'Where there's no love, must hatred fill the void?' I'll refer that one to the doctor.

BARTHOLO. What does that mean?

FIGARO. She'll tell you the whole story. (*Exits.*)

BARTHOLO (*watching him go*). That fool hasn't changed a bit. Mark my words, if they don't hang him first, he'll go to his grave the most arrogant, insolent . . .

MARCELINE (*turns to face him*). There you are, you see? That's you all over, doctor! You're so stiff and serious – a person might die waiting for your help, just as a certain couple got married not long ago, despite all your precautions.

BARTHOLO. And you're still nasty and sharp-tongued. Anyway, why is my presence at the castle so urgently required? Has His Lordship had an accident?

MARCELINE. No, doctor.

BARTHOLO. His deceitful Countess, my lady Rosine – perhaps she's unwell, praise God?

MARCELINE. She is out of sorts.

BARTHOLO. What's up with her?

MARCELINE. Her husband neglects her.

BARTHOLO (*delightedly*). Aha! So her noble spouse avenges me?

MARCELINE. I don't know how to describe the Count – he's both jealous *and* unfaithful.

BARTHOLO. Unfaithful from boredom, jealous from vanity – that's obvious enough.

MARCELINE. Today, for example, he's giving our Suzanne in marriage to his man Figaro, showing his favour through their union . . .

BARTHOLO. Which His Excellency has no doubt made necessary?

MARCELINE. Not quite. But it's a union His Excellency would very much like to enjoy in secret with the bride . . .

BARTHOLO. With Figaro's bride? I daresay he'll be able to make a deal with him.

MARCELINE. Not according to Bazile.

BARTHOLO. What, is that villain staying here too? A den of iniquity! What's he doing here?

MARCELINE. All the mischief he can think of. The most annoying thing, from my point of view, is this crush he's had on me for ages.

BARTHOLO. I'd put a stop to that with the greatest of ease.

MARCELINE. How?

BARTHOLO. By marrying him.

MARCELINE. You're a cruel wretch, making fun of me like that. Why didn't you put a stop to mine in the same way? Wasn't that what you should have done? Where's your memory for all those promises you made? And what became of our little Emmanuel, the fruit of that forgotten passion, which should have led us to the altar?

BARTHOLO (*taking off his hat*). Did you bring me here from Seville to listen to this sort of nonsense? And this sudden enthusiasm of yours for marriage . . .

MARCELINE. All right! We'll say no more about it. But if nothing could induce you to do the right thing and marry me, then at least help me to marry someone else.

BARTHOLO. With pleasure. Let's talk about it. But which mortal man, forsaken by God and woman alike . . . ?

MARCELINE. Eh? Why, who else could it be, doctor, but the handsome, kindhearted Figaro?

BARTHOLO. What, that scoundrel?

MARCELINE. Never angry, always in a good mood; living for the moment, caring as little about the future as the past; sparkling, and generous – oh, so generous . . .

BARTHOLO. Yes, like a thief.

MARCELINE. No, like a lord. In a word, he's the most charming man, but the most cruel monster!

BARTHOLO. And what about that Suzanne of his?

MARCELINE. She's not going to have him, the cunning wretch, if only you'll help me, dear doctor, to make good an obligation he already owes to me.

BARTHOLO. What, on the day of his wedding?

MARCELINE. People break these things off even later. And if I wasn't afraid of giving away a little feminine secret . . .

BARTHOLO. Do women have secrets from their doctors?

MARCELINE. Well, I have none from you, of course. Our sex is passionate, but timid. We are certainly drawn to pleasure, but even the most adventurous woman can hear a little voice within her that says: 'Be beautiful, if you can; be good, if you will; but be careful, since you must.' Now, since we must be careful, as every woman knows, let us first of all frighten the good Suzanne by threatening to disclose the offer being made to her.

BARTHOLO. And where will that lead?

MARCELINE. Well, she'll be overcome by shame, and continue to refuse the Count – and he, by way of revenge, will lend his weight to my objections to her marriage – accordingly, mine will be assured.

BARTHOLO. By God, she's right! That would be a clever trick – marrying off my old housekeeper to the rogue who lost me my young mistress!

MARCELINE. Yes, and who thinks he'll add to his pleasures by dashing my hopes.

BARTHOLO. And who robbed me once of a hundred crowns – that still preys on my mind.

MARCELINE. Oh, what bliss!

BARTHOLO. To punish a scoundrel . . .

MARCELINE. To marry him, Doctor, to marry him!

Enter SUZANNE, *carrying a hat with a broad ribbon in her hand, and a dress over her arm.*

SUZANNE. To marry him? Who are you talking about? My Figaro?

MARCELINE (*bitterly*). Why not? You're marrying him, aren't you?

BARTHOLO (*laughing*). Now for a good-going row between two angry women! We were just discussing, my dear Suzanne, the good fortune he'll enjoy in possessing you.

MARCELINE. And that's not counting His Lordship, whom we won't mention.

SUZANNE (*curtseying*). Your servant, madame. There's always a hint of bitterness in your remarks.

MARCELINE (*curtseying*). And I yours, madame. So where is the bitterness, pray? Isn't it only right that so liberal a gentleman should share a little of the happiness he procures for his servants?

SUZANNE. Procures?

MARCELINE. Yes, madame.

SUZANNE. Fortunately, madame's jealousy is as well known as her claims on Figaro are slight.

MARCELINE. I might have strengthened them, madame, had I chosen to cement them by the same methods as you.

SUZANNE. Oh, those methods, madame, are thoroughly familiar to any lady of experience.

MARCELINE. Which the dear child isn't, of course. Butter wouldn't melt in her mouth!

BARTHOLO (*dragging* MARCELINE *away*). Goodbye, master Figaro's pretty fiancée!

MARCELINE (*curtseying*). And His Lordship's secret little arrangement!

SUZANNE (*curtseying*). Who holds you in the highest esteem, madame.

MARCELINE (*curtseying*). Will she not also do me the honour of a little affection, madame?

SUZANNE (*curtseying*). In that respect, madame need desire nothing.

MARCELINE (*curtseying*). Madame is *so* pretty!

SUZANNE (*curtseying*). Indeed! Pretty enough to upset madame!

MARCELINE (*curtseying*). And above all, so respectable!

SUZANNE. That's something one leaves to mistresses.

MARCELINE (*outraged*). Mistresses! Mistresses!

BARTHOLO (*restraining her*). Marceline!

MARCELINE. Come along, Doctor, before I lose control of myself. Good day, madame. (*A curtsey.*)

Exit MARCELINE *and* BARTHOLO.

SUZANNE. Yes, clear off, madame! Pompous creature! And your attempts to insult me leave me cold. Just look at the old witch! Because she's had a bit of education, and made Her Ladyship's life hell when she was young, she thinks she can rule over the whole castle! (*She flings the dress she has been carrying onto a chair.*) Now I can't remember what I came in for.

CHÉRUBIN (*running in*). Ah, Suzanne, I've been waiting two hours to try and catch you on your own. Alas, you're getting married, and I'm leaving.

SUZANNE. What has my marriage got to do with His Lordship's favourite page leaving the castle?

CHÉRUBIN (*pathetically*). Suzanne, he's sending me away.

SUZANNE (*mimicking him*). Chérubin, have you been naughty again?

CHÉRUBIN. He caught me with your cousin Fanchette yesterday evening, when I was rehearsing her for the *ingénue* role she's playing tonight. He was absolutely furious. 'Get out of here,' he said, 'You little . . . ' I wouldn't dream of repeating the foul word he used in front of a lady. 'Get out, and you won't be sleeping in the castle tomorrow!' So unless Her Ladyship, my beautiful godmother, can manage to talk him round, it's all over, Suzanne – I'll be deprived forever of the pleasure of seeing you.

SUZANNE. Of seeing me? It's my turn now, is it? It's no longer my mistress you're secretly sighing for?

CHÉRUBIN. Oh, Suzanne, she's noble and beautiful, but she's so intimidating!

SUZANNE. Which is as much as to say that I'm not, so you can feel free to try . . .

CHÉRUBIN. Oh, you naughty creature, you know perfectly well I wouldn't dare try anything with you! But you're so fortunate! To see her at every moment of the day, to talk to her, to dress her in the morning and undress her at night, pin by pin . . . Oh, Suzanne! What I wouldn't give . . . What's that you have there?

SUZANNE (*teasing him*). Alas! It's the fortunate bonnet and the equally privileged ribbon that cover up your lovely godmother's hair for the night . . .

CHÉRUBIN (*excitedly*). Her ribbon! Oh, give it to me, please, my darling!

SUZANNE (*pulling it away*). Eh? Absolutely not! His darling, indeed! Getting quite familiar, isn't he. What a shame he's a no-account little wretch . . . ! (CHÉRUBIN *manages to snatch the ribbon from her.*) Oh! The ribbon!

CHÉRUBIN (*dodging behind a large armchair*). You can tell her it got torn or dirty, or that you've lost it. Tell her anything you like.

SUZANNE (*chasing after him*). Oh! In three or four years' time, mark my words – you'll be the worst scoundrel . . . ! Will you give me back that ribbon? (*Tries to take it back.*)

CHÉRUBIN (*pulls a songsheet from his pocket*). No, no, let me keep it, please, Suzanne! I'll let you have my ballad, and when the memory of your beautiful mistress saddens my every waking moment, the memory of you will be the one ray of sunshine which can still bring joy to my heart.

SUZANNE (*snatches the ballad from him*). Bring joy to your heart, you young rascal! You must think you're talking to that Fanchette of yours. You got caught with her, yet you're pining for Her Ladyship. And on top of all that, you're trying your luck with me!

CHÉRUBIN (*excitedly*). My word of honour, it's true! I don't know what's happening to me, but for some time now I've had the strangest feeling. My heart starts pounding at the very sight of a woman. The very words 'love' and 'desire' make it leap within my breast. Actually, I feel such a desperate need to say 'I love you' to someone, that I say it even when I'm by myself, walking in the park – to your mistress, to you, to the trees, to the clouds, to the wind which carries my words away, unheard. Yesterday I happened to meet Marceline . . . (SUZANNE *laughs*.) Well, why not? She's a woman, she's a girl! Woman! Girl! How sweet those words sound! How fascinating they are!

SUZANNE. He's gone mad!

CHÉRUBIN. Fanchette is nice – at least she listens to me, which is more than you do!

SUZANNE. Well, that's a pity, isn't it. Now you listen to me, sir! (*Tries to snatch the ribbon.*)

CHÉRUBIN (*dodges out of reach*). Aha! No, you don't! Over my dead body! And if that won't satisfy you, I'll add a thousand kisses to the price! (*Gives chase after her now.*)

SUZANNE (*evading him*). It'll be a thousand slaps, if you come any closer! I'll complain about this to my mistress, and so far from supporting you, I'll tell His Lordship myself: 'You've done the right thing, sir. Get rid of this little thief! Send him back to his parents, the nasty little creature – not content with pretending to be in love with Her Ladyship, he keeps trying to kiss me besides!"

CHÉRUBIN *catches sight of the* COUNT *entering; he flings himself behind the armchair in terror.*

CHÉRUBIN. I'm done for now!

SUZANNE. What's he frightened of? Ah!

SUZANNE *now sees the* COUNT, *goes over to the armchair to conceal* CHÉRUBIN.

COUNT (*goes up to her*). Ah, you're excited, my dear Suzanne! You're talking to yourself, and your little heart seems to be fluttering . . . Of course, that's understandable on a day like today.

SUZANNE (*anxiously*). What do you want with me, sir? If anyone were to find you here with me . . .

COUNT. I should be most upset if they did. However, you know the extent of my interest in you. Bazile has left you in no doubt as to my love for you. Suzanne, I have only a moment to explain my intentions – listen. (*He sits down on the armchair.*)

SUZANNE (*animatedly*). I'm not listening to anything.

COUNT (*takes her hand*). Just one word. You know that the King has appointed me his ambassador in London. I'm taking Figaro there with me. I'm giving him an excellent position, and since it is a wife's duty to follow her husband . . .

SUZANNE. Oh, if only I dared speak!

COUNT (*draws her closer to him*). Speak, my dear, speak! Exercise that right you hold over me now, and forever more!

SUZANNE (*alarmed*). I don't want any such right, sir – I don't want it. Let me go, please, I beg you.

COUNT. Then tell me, tell me first.

SUZANNE (*angrily*). I can't remember what I was going to say.

COUNT. About a wife's duty.

SUZANNE. Ah, yes. When His Lordship rescued his own wife from the Doctor, and married her for love – when for her sake he abolished a certain frightful *droit de seigneur* . . .

COUNT (*cheerfully*). Much to the annoyance of the girls! Oh, my dear Suzanne! What a pretty custom! Now, if you were to come and discuss it with me in the garden this evening, I would put such a price on that simple favour . . .

BAZILE (*off-stage*). He's not at home, sir.

COUNT (*stands up*). Whose voice is that?

SUZANNE. Oh, this is terrible!

COUNT. Go out now, in case someone comes in.

SUZANNE (*anxiously*). What, and leave you here?

BAZILE (*shouts off-stage*). His Lordship was with the Countess, he must have gone out. I'll go and see.

COUNT. And no place to hide! Ah! Behind this chair . . . it'll have to do, but get rid of him quickly.

SUZANNE *tries to bar his way; he pushes her gently, she steps back but still manages to place herself between him and the young page. However, as the* COUNT *crouches down,* CHÉRUBIN *jumps up and flings himself in terror onto the chair, kneeling, hiding his face.* SUZANNE *covers him up with the dress she is carrying, and stands in front of the chair.*

BAZILE. You haven't by any chance seen His Lordship, miss?

SUZANNE (*testily*). Eh? Why should I have seen him? Leave me alone.

BAZILE (*goes up to her*). Really, if you were more sensible, there would be nothing surprising about my question. It's Figaro who's looking for him.

SUZANNE. Then he's looking for his worst enemy, apart from yourself.

COUNT (*aside*). Now we'll see how well I'm being served.

BAZILE. What, to wish a woman well, means wanting to harm her husband?

SUZANNE. Indeed no, not by your frightful principles, an agent of corruption such as you.

BAZILE. What's being asked of you now, that you won't be giving away to somebody else anyway? Thanks to one pleasant little ceremony, what was forbidden to you yesterday, will be demanded of you tomorrow.

SUZANNE. Shameless creature!

BAZILE. Among serious matters, marriage is a pretty farcical affair, so what I had in mind was . . .

SUZANNE (*outraged*). Something horrible, yes! Who gave you permission to come in here?

BAZILE. Now, now, don't be nasty! Calm down, for heaven's sake. You won't have to do anything if you don't want to, but don't imagine that I regard Master Figaro as any obstacle to His Lordship. And as for that little page . . .

SUZANNE (*meekly*). What, Master Chérubin?

BAZILE (*mimicking her*). Yes, that *Cherubino di amore*, who chases after you incessantly, and who only this morning was prowling around outside, waiting to come in when I left you. Now, that's the truth, isn't it?

SUZANNE. What nonsense! Now, go away, you wicked man!

BAZILE. So, a person's wicked because he sees things clearly? This ballad of his, that he's being so secretive about – didn't he write it for you?

SUZANNE (*angrily*). Oh yes! For me, indeed!

BAZILE. That's of course if he didn't write it for Her Ladyship! Apparently he can't keep his eyes off her when he's serving at table. God forbid he should get up to any tricks in that direction! His Lordship is absolutely merciless on that point.

SUZANNE (*furiously*). And you're a vile wretch, going around spreading lies like that, to ruin a poor boy who's already in disgrace with his master!

BAZILE. So, I've made it up, have I? I'm only telling you what everyone else is saying.

COUNT (*stands up*). And just what *is* everyone else is saying!

SUZANNE. Heavens!

BAZILE. Ha! Ha!

COUNT. Go, Bazile, have him thrown out immediately.

BAZILE. Oh, dear! I wish now I hadn't come in.

SUZANNE (*upset*). Oh, my God! Oh, my God!

COUNT (*to* BAZILE). She's going to faint. Sit her down in this chair.

SUZANNE (*pushes him away vigorously*). No, I don't want to sit down. Just coming in like that, it's disgraceful!

COUNT. Well, there are two of us now, my dear. You're in no danger.

BAZILE. I'm sorry I made a joke about the page, I didn't know you were listening. I was only using him to try and discover her true feelings. Because deep down . . .

COUNT. Fifty crowns, a horse, and send him back to his parents.

BAZILE. But it was only a joke, sir.

COUNT. He's a lecherous young scoundrel – I've already caught him with the gardener's daughter.

BAZILE. With Fanchette?

COUNT. In her bedroom, no less.

SUZANNE (*outraged*). Where His Lordship no doubt also had some business!

COUNT (*delightedly*). I rather like that comment!

BAZILE. It's a good sign.

COUNT (*cheerfully*). Anyway, no. I went there to look for your uncle Antonio, that drunken gardener of mine, in order to give him some instructions. I knock, your cousin takes ages coming to the door, she looks embarrassed, and I become suspicious. I talk to her, and while we're chatting I have a look round. There's a sort of curtain behind the door, hiding some kind of wardrobe, I don't know. Anyway, without giving anything away, I lift this curtain up, gently, very gently (*Demonstrates by lifting up the dress covering the chair.*), and I see . . . (*He reveals* CHÉRUBIN.) Aha!

BAZILE. Ha! Ha!

COUNT. Just like the last time.

BAZILE. Even better.

COUNT (*to* SUZANNE). Well, this is wonderful, young lady! Barely engaged, and you're already making other arrangements. Was that why you wanted to be alone – so you could entertain my page? As for you, sir, this is typical of you – you have so little respect for your mistress that you chase after her maid, your own friend's future wife! But I will absolutely not permit Figaro, a man whom I love and admire, to be the victim of this kind of deception. Was he with you, Bazile?

SUZANNE (*indignantly*). There's no deception and no victim. He was there all the time you were talking to me.

COUNT (*furiously*). How can you tell such a barefaced lie! A man's worst enemy wouldn't wish him such misfortune.

SUZANNE. He was asking me to persuade Her Ladyship to intercede with you on his behalf. Then you appeared, and he was so terrified that he hid behind the chair.

COUNT (*angrily*). That's a damned fraud! I sat down in it when I came into the room.

CHÉRUBIN. Alas, sir, I was behind it, trembling with fear.

COUNT. More chicanery! I've just been behind there myself.

CHÉRUBIN. I beg your pardon, sir, but I was hiding *in* the chair then, covered up.

COUNT (*even more furiously*). This is a viper, this wretched little . . . a damned snake in the grass! He's heard every word!

CHÉRUBIN. On the contrary, sir, I was doing all I could not to hear a thing.

COUNT. Oh, treachery! (*To* SUZANNE.) You shall not marry Figaro!

BAZILE. Sir, have a care – someone's coming.

COUNT (*pulling* CHÉRUBIN *out of the chair and setting him on his feet*). Now, let him stand there for all the world to see!

Enter the COUNTESS, FIGARO, FANCHETTE, *and various servants and peasants all dressed in white.* FIGARO *is carrying a lady's toque, trimmed with white feathers and white ribbons, and is speaking to the* COUNTESS.

FIGARO. You are the only person who can obtain this favour for us, ma'am.

COUNTESS. You see how people are, my dear Count – they credit me with influence I do not possess. However, since what they are asking is not unreasonable . . .

COUNT (*discomfited*). It would have to be extremely reasonable, before . . .

FIGARO (*aside to* SUZANNE). Help me out here!

SUZANNE. It won't do any good.

FIGARO. Try, anyway.

COUNT (*to* FIGARO). Well? What is it you want?

FIGARO. My Lord, your vassals, who have been relieved by the abolition of a certain troublesome feudal right, which your love for Her Ladyship . . .

COUNT. Yes, well, that right no longer exists, so what are you trying to say?

FIGARO (*craftily*). That it's high time that the virtuous act of so fine a master was proclaimed to the world. And since it's of particular benefit to me today, I should like to be the first to celebrate it at my wedding.

COUNT (*even more discomfited*). You're quite wrong, my friend. The abolition of a shameful privilege is simply the cancellation of a debt to honesty. A Spaniard may wish to conquer beauty by his own efforts, but to demand the first night, the sweetest fruit of it, as a feudal imposition, well, that's the tyranny of a Vandal, not the right of a noble Castilian.

FIGARO (*taking* SUZANNE *by the hand*). Then permit this young person, who through your wisdom has preserved her honour, to receive from your own hand, publicly, this virginal crown, adorned with white feathers and ribbons, as a symbol of the purity of your intentions. Adopt this ceremony for all future marriages, and let these verses, sung in chorus, recall for ever the memory . . .

COUNT (*embarrassed*). If I didn't know that lover, poet, and musician are three titles licensing all kinds of folly . . .

FIGARO. Join with me, my friends!

ALL. My Lord! My Lord!

SUZANNE (*to the* COUNT). Why run away from a tribute you have so richly deserved?

COUNT (*aside*). Traitor!

FIGARO. Now, just look at her, My Lord. No more beautiful bride will ever demonstrate the magnitude of your sacrifice.

SUZANNE. Never mind my beauty, rather praise his virtue.

COUNT (*aside*). This is a clever trick.

COUNTESS. Let me join my voice to theirs, My Lord. This ceremony will always be precious to me, because it has its origin in the love you once bore me.

COUNT. And which I still do, Madame. On that account, I shall give way.

ALL. *Vivat!*

COUNT (*aside*). I'm trapped. (*Aloud.*) Just one thing – in order that the ceremony might be a little more widely publicised, let's postpone it until later. (*Aside.*) And let's find Marceline, quickly.

FIGARO (*to* CHÉRUBIN). Well, you mischievous imp, why aren't you cheering?

SUZANNE. He's in despair. His Lordship's sending him away.

COUNTESS. Oh, sir, let me beg pardon for him.

COUNT. He absolutely doesn't deserve it.

COUNTESS. But he's so young!

COUNT. Not as young as you think.

CHÉRUBIN (*trembling with fear*). Sir, the right to pardon generously wasn't the one you gave up when you married Her Ladyship.

COUNTESS. That's true – he only gave up something which harmed everybody.

SUZANNE. If His Lordship had given up his right to pardon, that would surely be the first he would wish to assume again in secret.

COUNT (*embarrassed*). Without a doubt.

COUNTESS. Then what's the point of assuming it again?

CHÉRUBIN (*to the* COUNT). I behaved foolishly, sir, it's true, but I never committed the least indiscretion in anything I said . . .

COUNT (*embarrassed*). Oh, all right, that's enough!

FIGARO. What does he mean?

COUNT (*animatedly*). Enough, enough! Everybody's demanding pardon for him, so I'll grant it. I'll go even further – I'll give him his own company in my regiment.

ALL. *Vivat!*

COUNT. But only on condition that he leaves this very instant to join it in Catalonia.

FIGARO. Oh, sir – tomorrow, surely.

COUNT (*firmly*). That is my wish.

CHÉRUBIN. And I shall obey it.

COUNT. Bid farewell to your godmother, and ask her to pray for you.

CHÉRUBIN *goes down on one knee before the* COUNTESS, *but is unable to speak.*

COUNTESS (*deeply moved*). Since we can't keep you here even for just today, then go, young man. A new calling beckons you – go, and fulfil it worthily. Be a credit to your benefactor. Remember this house, where your youth was so greatly favoured. Be obedient, honourable and brave. We shall rejoice in your successes.

CHÉRUBIN *stands up and returns to his place.*

COUNT. You are obviously moved, Madame!

COUNTESS. I won't deny it. Who knows what fate awaits a young boy thrown into such a dangerous career? He's a relative of mine, and my godson, what's more.

COUNT (*aside*). I can see Bazile was right. (*Aloud.*) Now, young man – you may kiss Suzanne . . . for the last time.

FIGARO. Why so, my Lord? He'll be coming back to spend the winters here. Kiss me too, Captain! (*Embraces him.*) Farewell, my little Chérubin. You're going to lead a very different life, my lad. Dammit, yes! No more chasing after the girls all day, no more buns and cream cakes, no more tag or blind-man's-buff. Just brave soldiers, by God! Sunburnt, raggedy-arsed, a rifle that weighs a ton. Right turn! Left turn! Forward march to glory! Stick to the road and don't waver, unless a good burst of shot . . .

SUZANNE. Oh, horrors, that's enough!

COUNTESS. What a prospect!

COUNT. Where is Marceline? It's most peculiar that she's not here with you.

FANCHETTE. She's gone into town, My Lord, by the little farm track.

COUNT. And she'll be coming back? . . .

BAZILE. When God pleases.

FIGARO. If only it would please Him to make it never . . .

FANCHETTE. The Doctor was with her.

COUNT (*quickly*). The Doctor's here, is he?

BAZILE. She grabbed him the moment he arrived.

COUNT (*aside*). He couldn't have come at a better time.

FANCHETTE. She looked very annoyed about something. She was shouting while they were walking, then she stopped and did like this, waving her arms, and then the Doctor did like this, with his hand, trying to calm her down. She looked absolutely furious, and kept mentioning my cousin Figaro.

COUNT (*rubbing his chin*). Future cousin . . .

FANCHETTE (*indicating* CHÉRUBIN). Sir, have you forgiven us for yesterday? . . .

COUNT (*interrupting her*). Yes, yes, my dear, of course.

FIGARO. It's her damnable love for me that's bothering her. She would have made trouble at our wedding.

COUNT (*aside*). She'll make trouble all right – I'll see to that. (*Aloud.*) Now then, Madame, shall we go in? Bazile, come to my room.

SUZANNE (*to* FIGARO). Will you come back with me, my dear?

FIGARO (*aside to* SUZANNE). Have we caught him out nicely?

SUZANNE (*aside*). Clever boy!

Exit ALL. *As they are going out,* FIGARO *detains* CHÉRUBIN *and* BAZILE *and brings them back in.*

FIGARO. Now, listen, you two. Once the ceremony's over, there are my celebrations to come this evening. Let's run through what we plan to do – we don't want to be like those actors who perform at their worst when the critics are at their sharpest. We won't be able to make up for it tomorrow, so let's know our parts thoroughly today.

BAZILE (*meaningfully*). Mine's more difficult than you think.

FIGARO (*making a gesture, unseen by Bazile, as if to punch him*). Ah, but you have no idea the reward it'll bring you.

CHÉRUBIN. You forget I'm leaving, my friend.

FIGARO. And wouldn't you rather stay?

CHÉRUBIN. Oh, if only I could!

FIGARO. We have to apply a bit of trickery here. Don't say a word of complaint about your having to leave. Put your travelling coat over your shoulder, organise all your packing quite openly, and let them see your horse at the gate. Gallop as far as the farm, then return on foot by the back way. His Lordship will think you've left – just keep out of sight, and leave it to me, I'll talk him round after the celebrations.

CHÉRUBIN. But what about Fanchette? She doesn't know her part!

BAZILE. Then what the devil have you been teaching her, sir? You've been with her a whole week!

FIGARO. You've nothing else to do today. You can give her a free lesson.

BAZILE. Take care, young man, take care! Her father's far from pleased. The girl's already had her ears boxed, and it's not studying she's been doing with you. Oh, Chérubin, Chérubin, you'll get into serious trouble one of these days. The pitcher can only go to the well so often, you know . . .

FIGARO. Will you listen to the old fool and his ancient proverbs! All right, master, what does the wisdom of the ages tell us? The pitcher can only go to the well so often, and then what? . . .

BAZILE. It gets filled up.

FIGARO (*making to exit*). That's not bad. That's not bad at all.

Curtain.

ACT TWO

The scene is a luxuriously furnished bedroom, with a large bed in a recess, and a raised platform in front of it. There is a door upstage right, and another leading to a small closet downstage left. The door to the women's rooms is upstage, and there is a window at the other side. SUZANNE *and the* COUNTESS *enter right.*

COUNTESS (*flinging herself into an easy-chair*). Now, close the door, Suzanne, and tell me what happened, every last detail.

SUZANNE. Ma'am, I've kept nothing back from you.

COUNTESS. What? You really mean he was trying to seduce you, Suzanne?

SUZANNE. Oh, no. His Lordship wouldn't go to all that bother with one of his servants. No, he wanted to buy me.

COUNTESS. And the young page was in the room?

SUZANNE. He was indeed, hidden behind the armchair. He'd come to ask me if I would persuade you to speak up for him.

COUNTESS. And why couldn't he have come to me himself? How could I have refused him, Suzanne?

SUZANNE. That's what I told him. But he was so upset at having to leave, and especially at parting from Your Ladyship. 'Oh, Suzanne, she's so noble and beautiful! But she's so intimidating!'

COUNTESS. Is that really how I appear, Suzanne? And I've always looked after him, too.

SUZANNE. Then he caught sight of your ribbon, which I had in my hand, and he practically threw himself at it!

COUNTESS (*smiling*). My ribbon? How childish.

SUZANNE. I tried to get it back from him, but he was like a lion, ma'am, his eyes blazing! 'Over my dead body!' he said, trying to force that little squeaky voice of his.

COUNTESS (*dreamily*). And then, Suzanne?

SUZANNE. Well, ma'am, what can you make of a young devil like that? On the one hand, respect for his godmother, but on the other – oh, if only . . . And because he daren't even kiss the hem of Your Ladyship's gown, he wanted to kiss me, if you like!

COUNTESS (*dreamily*). That'll do . . . enough of these follies. So, my dear Suzanne, what did my husband eventually say?

SUZANNE. That if I wouldn't do what he wanted, he would take Marceline's side.

COUNTESS (*gets up and walks round the room, rapidly fanning herself*). He doesn't love me any more.

SUZANNE. Then why is he so jealous?

COUNTESS. He's like all husbands, my dear – it's his pride, nothing else. Ah! I've loved him too much. I've wearied him with my affection, and tired him out with my love. That's the only wrong I've done him. However, I don't intend to let you suffer for this honest confession, and you shall marry Figaro. He's the only one who can help us. Is he coming back?

SUZANNE. As soon as he's seen off the hunt.

COUNTESS (*fanning herself*). Open the window a little. It's so hot in here.

SUZANNE. That's because you're pacing up and down, ma'am.

She opens the window upstage.

COUNTESS (*dreamily*). If only he didn't keep trying to avoid me . . . Men really are impossible!

SUZANNE (*shouts from the window*). Ah! There's His Lordship now, ma'am, coming through the kitchen garden, with Pédrille behind him and two or three – no, four greyhounds.

COUNTESS. Then we still have some time. (*Sits down.*) Is that someone knocking, Suzanne?

SUZANNE (*runs to open the door, singing*). Ah, it's my Figaro! It's my Figaro! Do come in, my dear – Her Ladyship's most anxious to see you!

FIGARO (*entering*). And what about you, my dear little Suzanne? Anyway, Her Ladyship needn't worry. After all, what are we talking about? A mere bagatelle. His Lordship finds a certain young woman attractive, he wishes to make her his mistress – what could be more natural?

SUZANNE. Natural?

FIGARO. Accordingly, he appoints me his courier, and Suzanne his *chargé d'affaires*. He's not stupid, is he.

SUZANNE. Have you done?

FIGARO. And because Suzanne, my fiancée, won't accept the commission, he decides to use his influence on behalf of Marceline – again, what could be simpler? You take your revenge on people who upset your little schemes by upsetting theirs. That's what everyone else does, and that's what we're going to do. That's all there is to it.

COUNTESS. Figaro, how can you be so flippant about a plot which could cost all of us our happiness?

FIGARO. Who says that, ma'am?

SUZANNE. Well, I mean, instead of showing some concern for our distress . . .

FIGARO. I'm dealing with it – isn't that enough? Anyway, if we're going to act as methodically as His Lordship, let's first of all cool his ardour for what's ours, by making him worry about what's his.

COUNTESS. That's easily said, but how do we do that?

FIGARO. It's already done, ma'am. A false report on yourself . . .

COUNTESS. On me! Have you gone mad?

FIGARO. No, but *he* must!

COUNTESS. A man as jealous as the Count . . . !

FIGARO. So much the better. If you're trying to put one over on someone with a bit of spirit, you need to get their blood up. Women know that well! Make a man angry enough, and with a little skulduggery you can lead him by the nose, right into the Guadalquivir! I've arranged for Bazile to receive an anonymous note, warning His Lordship that a young man is planning to meet you at the ball tonight.

COUNTESS. And you're going to play tricks with the truth, concerning an honest woman! . . .

FIGARO. Ma'am, there aren't many I would take that risk with, in case it might turn out to be true.

COUNTESS. And I'm supposed to be grateful!

FIGARO. But tell me, ma'am – isn't it nice of me to have arranged his day for him, so that he'll spend his time prowling around cursing his own wife, instead of amusing himself with mine? He's already upset – running all over the place, not sure whether to follow her or spy on her. In his troubled mind, just look at him, tearing across country after a few pathetic hares. It'll soon be time for the wedding, and he'll have done nothing to stop it. And he won't dare to oppose it in front of Your Ladyship.

SUZANNE. No, but Marceline, she's smart enough – she will.

FIGARO. Hah! As if that worries me. You just tell His Lordship that you'll meet him at dusk in the garden.

SUZANNE. You're still counting on that?

FIGARO. Oh, for God's sake! Listen – people who don't try never achieve anything, and never come to anything. That's my opinion.

SUZANNE. That's very nice!

COUNTESS. Huh, like this idea of his. Are you actually going to let her go?

FIGARO. No, of course not. I'll get somebody to put on one of Suzanne's dresses. And when we surprise the Count at the rendezvous, how will he talk his way out of it?

SUZANNE. So who's going to wear my clothes?

FIGARO. Chérubin.

COUNTESS. But he's gone.

FIGARO. Not to my knowledge. Now, will you leave all this to me, ma'am?

SUZANNE. If it involves scheming, we can rely on him.

FIGARO. Two, three, four threads at the same time – all tangled up and criss-crossing. I should have been a courtier!

SUZANNE. People say it's a difficult job.

FIGARO. Getting, taking, and asking – that's the secret in three words.

COUNTESS. He has so much confidence, he even inspires it in me.

FIGARO. That's my intention.

SUZANNE. Anyway, you were saying . . .

FIGARO. I was saying that while His Lordship is away, I'll send Chérubin to you. You can do his hair and dress him – I'll take him aside and instruct him – then it's 'Dance, Your Lordship, dance!' (*Exits.*)

COUNTESS (*sitting, with her beauty-box in her hand*). Heavens, Suzanne, I look a fright! This young man who'll be coming . . .

SUZANNE. Ma'am, you're not going to let him off?

COUNTESS (*dreamily, looking into her hand-mirror*). Me? No, just wait and see how I'll scold him.

SUZANNE. Let's make him sing his ballad. (*Places it on the* COUNTESS's *lap.*)

COUNTESS. You know, my hair's an absolute mess . . .

SUZANNE (*laughing*). I've only to fix a couple of curls, ma'am – then you'll be able to scold him much better.

COUNTESS (*lost in thought*). What was that you said?

Enter CHÉRUBIN, *sheepishly.*

SUZANNE. Come in, Officer Chérubin – Madame is at home!

CHÉRUBIN (*approaches nervously*). Oh, the pain that word causes me, ma'am! It reminds me that I must go from this place . . . leaving behind a godmother . . . one so . . . one so kind!

SUZANNE. And so beautiful!

CHÉRUBIN (*with a sigh*). Ah, yes!

SUZANNE (*mimicking him*). Ah, yes! What a fine young man – with those sly downcast eyes! Come on, my handsome little bluebird – sing your ballad for Her Ladyship.

COUNTESS (*unfolding it*). So tell me – who is it about?

SUZANNE. Look, he's blushing – he's gone bright red!

CHÉRUBIN. Is it forbidden to care for someone?

SUZANNE (*shoves her fist under his nose*). I'll tell everything, you wretch!

COUNTESS. So, is he going to sing?

CHÉRUBIN. Oh, ma'am – I'm so shy! . . .

SUZANNE (*laughing*). There, there – poor little thing . . .
The minute Her Ladyship wants to hear it, you come
over all bashful! Go on, I'll accompany you.

COUNTESS. Take my guitar.

The COUNTESS *sits, following the music from the manuscript.*
SUZANNE *plays the guitar behind her armchair, reading the
accompaniment over her mistress' shoulder.* CHÉRUBIN *stands
facing her, his eyes lowered. The whole scene recalls the splendid
print, after Vanloo, titled 'Conversation espagnole'.*

CHÉRUBIN (*to the tune of 'Malbrough s'en va-t-en guerre'*).
My noble steed was weary
(And my heart, my heart filled with sorrow!)
As we crossed the plain so dreary,
And whither who can say?

And whither who can say?
No friend to cheer my way
And by a fountain shady,
(Ah, my heart, my heart filled with sorrow!)
I thought upon my lady,
And down my tears did rain.

And down my tears did rain,
My body wracked with pain.
Upon a tree all entwined,
(Ah, my heart, my heart filled with sorrow!)
I carved her name and mine,
Just as the King rode by.

Just as the King rode by,
With his lords and ladies high.
'Oh, tell me, page,' said the Queen,
(Ah, my heart, my heart filled with sorrow!)

What causes thee such pain?
Why art thou in distress?'

'Why art thou in distress?
Come, pretty page, confess.
My heart, alas, is heavy,
(Ah, my heart, my heart filled with sorrow!)
For I must leave my lady,
Whom I shall love for aye.'

'Whom I shall love for aye,
Until the day I die.'
'O, pretty page,' said the Queen,
(Ah, my heart, my heart filled with sorrow!)
'Have you none kinder seen?
I shall her place supply.'

'I shall her place supply,
And you shall no more sigh,
For to my Captain's daughter
(Ah, my heart, my heart filled with sorrow!)
You shall be wed hereafter –
You will not me deny.'

'You will not me deny.'
'No, Majesty, not I,
For I must bear my pain
(Ah, my heart, my heart filled with sorrow!)
By love till death enchained,
My tears no-one can dry.'

COUNTESS. It has a certain naïve charm . . . a good deal of feeling.

SUZANNE (*puts the guitar down on a chair*). Oh, yes – when it comes to feeling, this is a young man who . . . Anyway,

my brave sir, have you been told how we plan to
brighten up this evening? We need to try one of my
dresses on you, to see if it'll fit.

COUNTESS. I doubt if it will.

SUZANNE (*measures herself against him*). Well, he's about my
height. Let's take his coat off first. (*Removes his coat.*)

COUNTESS. What if someone comes in?

SUZANNE. So? What harm are we doing? I'll go and shut
the door. (*Runs to do so.*) It's his hair I want to look at.

COUNTESS. On my dressing-table – there's a bonnet of
mine. (*Exit SUZANNE to the closet off-stage.*) Now, up to
the point when the ball commences, the Count won't
know you're still in the castle. We'll tell him afterwards
that it was because you had to wait for your commission
to be made out, and that's what gave us the idea . . .

CHÉRUBIN (*showing it to her*). Alas, ma'am, I have it here!
Bazile handed it to me personally.

COUNTESS. Already? They obviously didn't want to lose
any time. (*Reads it.*) Hm . . . they've been in such a hurry
they've forgotten to put the seal on it. (*Hands it back to him.*)

SUZANNE (*re-entering with a large bonnet*). The seal on what?

COUNTESS. On his commission.

SUZANNE. He has it already?

COUNTESS. Yes, that's what I was saying. Is that my
bonnet?

SUZANNE (*sits down beside the COUNTESS*). It's the
prettiest one you have, ma'am. (*She begins singing, with pins
in her mouth.*)

'Turn and face me, darling boy,
Bel ami, you're all my joy . . . '

CHÉRUBIN *kneels before her, while she does his hair.*

Oh, ma'am, isn't he charming!

COUNTESS. Fix his collar – make him look a little more feminine.

SUZANNE (*adjusts it*). There! Just look at the little scamp – doesn't he make a lovely girl? I'm jealous, I tell you! (*Takes him by the chin.*) Wouldn't you like to be as pretty as this?

COUNTESS. Honestly, she's quite mad! Now, we'd better tuck up the sleeve and fasten the cuff. (*Pulls up his sleeve.*) What's this round your wrist? A ribbon!

SUZANNE. Yes, and it's one of yours, ma'am. I'm very pleased Your Ladyship has seen it. I told him I was going to tell you. And if His Lordship hadn't come in, I'd have got the ribbon back – I'm practically as strong as he is.

COUNTESS. Why, there's blood on it! (*She takes the ribbon off.*)

CHÉRUBIN (*shamefaced*). That was this morning – I thought I was leaving, and I was fastening my horse's curb-chain. He tossed his head, and the bit grazed my arm.

COUNTESS. But you wouldn't use a ribbon to . . .

SUZANNE. Especially not a stolen ribbon. Anyway, what's all this about curbs and bits – these horsey things, I don't understand a word of it . . . Oh, look how white his arm is – it's like a woman's. It's whiter than mine! Look, ma'am, look! (*She compares them.*)

COUNTESS (*coldly*). You'd do better to fetch the sticking-plaster from my dressing-room.

SUZANNE *laughs and pushes* CHÉRUBIN's *head away. He falls over onto his hands. She exits to the closet off-stage. The* COUNTESS *remains silent a few moments, looking at her ribbon.* CHÉRUBIN *devours her with his eyes.*

As for my ribbon, sir . . . since the colour of this one particularly suits me, I should have been very upset to lose it.

SUZANNE (*re-entering*). Now, what about a bandage for his arm? (*She hands the* COUNTESS *the sticking-plaster and scissors.*)

COUNTESS. You can take the ribbon out of another bonnet, while you're looking out some clothes for him. (*Exit* SUZANNE *by the upstage door, carrying* CHÉRUBIN's *coat.*)

CHÉRUBIN (*his eyes lowered, still kneeling*). The one that's been taken away from me would have cured it in no time.

COUNTESS. In what way? (*Showing him the sticking-plaster.*) This is better.

CHÉRUBIN (*shyly*). When a ribbon . . . has bound the hair . . . or touched the skin of a certain person . . .

COUNTESS (*cutting him off*). Someone whom you don't even know, it cures all ills, does it? Well, that's news to me, but I'll put it to the test. I'll keep the ribbon you tied round your arm, and at the first sign of a scratch . . . on one of my maids, I'll try it out.

CHÉRUBIN (*saddened*). You're going to keep it, and I must leave!

COUNTESS. Not for ever.

CHÉRUBIN. I'm so unhappy.

COUNTESS. Now he's crying! It's that wretch Figaro's fault, and his stories about the army!

CHÉRUBIN (*exalted*). Oh, if only I could meet the kind of glorious end he prophesied for me! If I were assured of sudden death, then perhaps my lips would dare to utter . . .

COUNTESS (*interrupts him and dries his eyes with her handkerchief*). Be quiet, child, be quiet! You're making no sense whatsoever. (*A knock at the door. She calls out.*) What's all that knocking?

COUNT (*off-stage*). Why is this door locked?

COUNTESS (*alarmed, stands up*). It's my husband! Oh, my God! (*To* CHÉRUBIN, *now also on his feet.*) Look at you – you've no coat, your neck and arms are bare, and you're alone here with me! Everything's a mess – he'll have that letter now, and he's so jealous!

COUNT (*off-stage*). Unlock the door, will you?

COUNTESS. It's . . . it's because I'm alone.

COUNT (*off-stage*). Alone? Who's that you're talking with?

COUNTESS (*desperately*). Why, you, of course.

CHÉRUBIN (*aside*). After yesterday and this morning's goings-on, he'll kill me on the spot!

He runs into the closet and pulls the door shut behind him. The COUNTESS *takes out her key and hurries to admit the* COUNT.

COUNTESS. Oh, this is terrible! Terrible!

COUNT (*rather sharply*). Since when have you been in the habit of locking yourself in?

COUNTESS (*agitated*). I . . . I was sewing . . . yes, I was sewing along with Suzanne. She's just gone to her room for a moment.

COUNT (*peers closely at her*). There's something odd about you – you look different.

COUNTESS. Well, that's not surprising . . . not in the least . . . in fact, we were just talking about you, and she went to her room, as I said . . .

COUNT. Oh, you were talking about me, were you? Well, I've come back because I was worried. I was just about to mount my horse, and someone handed me a letter. Frankly, I don't believe a word of it, but I'm concerned all the same.

COUNTESS. What do you mean, sir? What letter?

COUNT. The fact is, Madame, that there are some mischievous people around. I've been warned that at some point today, a certain individual whom I believed to be gone, plans to seek a rendezvous with you.

COUNTESS. Well, no matter how daring he is, he'll have to break in, since I've no intention of leaving my room today.

COUNT. What about this evening – for Suzanne's wedding?

COUNTESS. Not for anything. I'm not feeling too well.

COUNT. Hm . . . fortunately the doctor's here. (CHÉRUBIN *knocks over a chair in the closet.*) What's that noise?

COUNTESS (*alarmed*). What noise?

COUNT. Someone's knocked over a chair.

COUNTESS. I . . . I didn't hear anything.

COUNT. You must be extremely preoccupied!

COUNTESS. Preoccupied? With what?

COUNT. There's someone in that room, Madame.

COUNTESS. What? Now, who on earth could it be, sir?

COUNT. That's what I'm asking you. I've only just come in.

COUNTESS. Well, Suzanne, presumably – she must be looking for something.

COUNT. But you've just told me she'd gone to her own room!

COUNTESS. Well, yes, that's right – or perhaps in there. I'm not sure which.

COUNT. If it's Suzanne, why are you so obviously concerned?

COUNTESS. Concerned about my maid?

COUNT. Whether it's about your maid or not, I don't know, but you're concerned about something, that's for sure.

COUNTESS. What's for sure, sir, is that this young woman concerns you, and interests you, far more than I do!

COUNT (*angrily*). She interests me to such an extent, Madame, that I wish to see her this very instant!

COUNTESS. Yes, indeed, I've no doubt you do, and often, but these suspicions of yours are ill-founded.

SUZANNE *pushes open the upstage door, carrying some dresses.*

COUNT. Then they'll be all the easier to dismiss, won't they. (*Looks towards the dressing-room and calls out.*) Suzanne! Come on out, I'm ordering you! (SUZANNE *pauses upstage beside the alcove.*)

COUNTESS. Sir, she's got practically nothing on. Do you normally burst in on women like this? She was trying on some dresses I'd given her as a wedding present. She ran out as soon as she heard you coming.

COUNT. Well, if she's afraid to show herself, she can surely talk. (*Turns towards the dressing-room door.*) Answer me, Suzanne – are you in that room? (SUZANNE *remains upstage, darts into the alcove and hides.*)

COUNTESS (*quickly, turning to the dressing-room*). Suzanne, I forbid you to answer! (*To the* COUNT.) This is the last word in tyranny!

COUNT (*goes up to the dressing-room door*). Very well, if she won't speak – I'll have a look at her, clothed or unclothed!

COUNTESS (*stands in front of him*). No! Anywhere else I couldn't prevent this, but I should hope that in my own room . . .

COUNT. And I should hope to discover who this mysterious Suzanne is, right now! I can see it's pointless asking you for the key, but it won't take much to break down this flimsy door! Hello! Somebody!

COUNTESS. That's right, call your servants! Cause a public scandal, and make us the talk of the castle!

COUNT. Very well, Madame. I can do the job myself – I'll go right now and get what I need . . . (*Makes to exit, then comes back.*) But so that everything remains just as it is, will you be so good as to accompany me, without any fuss or scandal, since you find that so unpleasant? It's a simple enough request – you surely won't refuse me?

COUNTESS (*uneasy*). Oh, sir – who would dream of refusing you anything?

COUNT. Ah, yes – I almost forgot the door to the maids' quarters. That'll have to be locked too, so you can prove your complete innocence. (*He goes to lock the upstage door and removes the key.*)

COUNTESS (*aside*). God, this is so stupid!

COUNT (*rejoining her*). Now that the bedroom is sealed, I should be obliged if you would take my arm . . . (*Raising his voice.*) And as for Suzanne – she of the dressing-room – she will of course have the goodness to wait for me. And if the slightest harm should befall her before my return . . .

COUNTESS. Really, sir, this is the most hateful business . . .

The COUNT *ushers her out and locks the door behind them.* SUZANNE *emerges from the alcove, hurries over to the dressing-room and speaks to* CHÉRUBIN *through the keyhole.*

SUZANNE. Chérubin, open the door, quickly! It's Suzanne! Open up and come out!

CHÉRUBIN (*comes out*). Oh, Suzanne! What a dreadful carry-on!

SUZANNE. Go, go! You haven't a minute to lose!

CHÉRUBIN (*frightened*). Go where?

SUZANNE. I don't know – just go!

CHÉRUBIN. But what if there's no way out?

SUZANNE. Listen, after that last little encounter, he'd beat you to a pulp, and that'd be the end of all of us! Run and tell Figaro what's happened . . .

CHÉRUBIN. Maybe it's not too far down to the garden . . . (*Runs to the window and looks out.*)

SUZANNE (*horrified*). It's two storeys up! Impossible! Oh, my poor mistress! And my marriage, oh God!

CHÉRUBIN. It's right over the melon-patch – at the risk of squashing a few . . . .

SUZANNE (*holding him back, shrieks*). He's going to kill himself!

CHÉRUBIN (*exalted*). Into the fiery furnace, Suzanne! Yes, rather than let any harm come to her . . . And this kiss will bring me luck! (*Kisses her, runs to the window and leaps out.*)

SUZANNE *cries out in alarm, and slumps into a chair. After a moment she crosses apprehensively to the window and looks out, then returns.*

SUZANNE. Ah! He's already out of sight. The young rascal! As nimble as he is handsome! If he ever lacks for women . . . I'd better take his place as quickly as possible. (*Going into the dressing-room.*) Well, Your Lordship, you can break the door down now if you like, but you'll get devil a word out of me! (*Locks herself in.*)

The COUNT *and* COUNTESS *come back into the room. He is carrying a crowbar, which he flings onto the chair.*

COUNT. Everything's just as I left it. Madame, before you force me to break open this door, consider the consequences. Once again – will you unlock it?

COUNTESS. Oh, sir, you've changed terribly! What causes someone to destroy a relationship like this? If these rages of yours were prompted by love, then I might excuse them, despite their absurdity. I might ignore the fact that they are insulting to me, if that were the reason. But can sheer vanity drive a man of honour to such excess?

COUNT. Love or vanity, if you don't open that door this instant, I'll . . .

COUNTESS (*barring his way*). Stop, sir, I beg you! Do you honestly believe me so lacking in self-respect?

COUNT. I'll believe anything you like, Madame, but I am going to see who's in that room!

COUNTESS (*alarmed*). Very well, sir – you shall see. But first, listen to me . . . and keep calm.

COUNT. So, it isn't Suzanne after all?

COUNTESS (*timidly*). Well . . . at least it's not someone . . . you need have no fear of this person . . . We were preparing a little joke . . . entirely innocent, it's the truth, for this evening . . . and I swear to you, sir . . .

COUNT. You swear to me . . . ?

COUNTESS. That neither he nor I had the slightest intention of offending you.

COUNT (*quickly*). Neither he nor I? So it's a man?

COUNTESS. A boy, sir.

COUNT. Ha! And who is it?

COUNTESS. Oh, sir, I hardly dare say his name!

COUNT. I'll kill him!

COUNTESS. Good God!

COUNT. Tell me!

COUNTESS. It's . . . it's young Chérubin . . .

COUNT. Chérubin! That impudent wretch! That explains all my suspicions, and the letter!

COUNTESS (*wringing her hands*). Oh, sir! You surely don't think . . .

COUNT (*stamping his foot. Aside*). This damned page! He's everywhere I go! (*Aloud.*) Right, Madame, open the door – I know the whole story now. You wouldn't have been so upset this morning, bidding him farewell – you wouldn't have made up that whole cock-and-bull story about Suzanne – and he wouldn't have taken such care to conceal himself, if there was nothing criminal in all this!

COUNTESS. He was afraid to show himself, in case you'd be annoyed.

COUNT (*enraged, shouts at the dressing-room door*). Come out here, you miserable creature!

COUNTESS (*catches him round the waist and pulls him away*). Oh, sir! Sir! You're so angry – I'm terrified for him! Please don't trust to suspicion, I beg you! And just because he's not properly dressed . . .

COUNT. Not properly dressed!

COUNTESS. Alas, yes! He was getting ready to dress up as a woman, with one of my bonnets on his head . . . he has no coat on, and his shirt's open at the neck . . . his arms are bare, too. He was just about to try on . . .

COUNT. And you were supposed to be staying in your room all day! Hah! You're not fit to be a wife! Well, you'll stay in your room all right – a very long time! But first, I have to kick an impudent scoundrel out of it, and make damned sure he's never seen again!

COUNTESS (*falls to her knees, her arms raised imploringly*). My Lord, I beg you, spare the boy! I'd never forgive myself if I were the cause of . . .

COUNT. Your fears only make his crime worse.

COUNTESS. It's not his fault, he was leaving – it was I who had him recalled.

COUNT (*furious*). Get up! Get out of my way! You have the nerve to plead on another man's behalf!

COUNTESS. Very well! I'll go, sir. I'll stand up and go. I'll even give you the key to the room. But in the name of your love . . .

COUNT. My love! You perfidious creature!

COUNTESS (*stands up and hands him the key*). Promise me that you'll let that boy go without harming him. After that, you can vent your rage on me, if I can't convince you that . . .

COUNT (*taking the key*). I don't want to hear another word.

The COUNTESS *flings herself on a couch, a handkerchief to her eyes.*

COUNTESS. Oh, my God – he's going to kill him!

The COUNT *opens the door and instantly recoils.*

COUNT. Suzanne!

SUZANNE *emerges, laughing.*

SUZANNE. 'I'll kill him! I'll kill him!' Well, go on, kill this wicked page!

COUNT (*aside*). Ah! I've been tricked! (*Looking at the astonished* COUNTESS.) And you too – feigning surprise, eh? Well, maybe she isn't alone in there . . . (*Goes into the dressing-room.*)

SUZANNE (*runs up to the* COUNTESS). You can relax, ma'am – he's miles away. He jumped out of the . . .

COUNTESS. Oh, Suzanne! I'm as good as dead!

The COUNT *emerges from the dressing-room, bewildered.*

COUNT (*after a brief silence*). There's no-one there. It seems I'm mistaken. Madame? You play your part extremely well.

SUZANNE (*merrily*). And what about me, Your Lordship?

The COUNTESS, *covering her mouth with her handkerchief while she regains her composure, says nothing. The* COUNT *goes up to her.*

COUNT. So, you were having a little joke, Madame?

COUNTESS (*recovering a little*). Well, why not, sir?

COUNT. A pretty damnable joke. What's the point of it, I'd like to know?

COUNTESS. What, d'you think your silliness deserves any sympathy?

COUNT. Silliness, you call it, when it concerns my honour?

COUNTESS (*growing more and more confident*). Did I marry you in order to be forever the victim of neglect, and jealousy, which you dare to justify on the grounds of . . .

COUNT. Madame, you're being too severe.

SUZANNE. Her Ladyship could easily have let you go ahead and call the servants.

COUNT. You're right, and I should feel deeply humble . . . I'm sorry, my mind's in a whirl . . .

SUZANNE. Admit it, Your Lordship, you did rather deserve it!

COUNT. So why didn't you come out when I called you? You wicked creature!

SUZANNE. I was doing my best to put my clothes back on, with all those pins. Anyway, Her Ladyship had forbidden me, with very good reason.

COUNT. Instead of harping on about my faults, you'd do better to help me make peace with her.

COUNTESS. No, sir! There can be no excuse for an outrage of this kind. I shall go into a convent, and not before time, either.

COUNT. Could you honestly do that, without some regrets?

SUZANNE. I'm sure there'd be many a tear shed, ma'am, the day you were to leave.

COUNTESS. Hah! I very much doubt it, Suzanne. And I'd rather live with my regrets than the humiliation of forgiving him. He's hurt me too deeply.

COUNT. Rosine!

COUNTESS. No! I'm no longer that same Rosine you once pursued so eagerly! I am poor Countess Almaviva, the sad neglected wife, whom you no longer love.

SUZANNE. Madame!

COUNT (*pleading*). For pity's sake!

COUNTESS. Pity? You had none for me.

COUNT. But there was that letter . . . it made my blood boil!

COUNTESS. I didn't give permission to anyone to write it.

COUNT. You knew about it?

COUNTESS. It was that idiot Figaro . . .

COUNT. He was involved in it?

COUNTESS. . . . who gave it to Bazile.

COUNT. Who told me he got it from some peasant. That treacherous dog of a music master! Well, sir, it's a double-edged sword, and *you'll* pay for everybody!

COUNTESS. You see? You ask pardon for yourself, and deny it to others – that's men all over! Well, if I were to agree to pardon your offence, on the grounds that you were provoked by that letter, then I'd demand a general amnesty.

COUNT. With all my heart, Madame. But how can I atone for so shameful a fault?

COUNTESS (*stands up*). The fault was on both sides.

COUNT. Ah, no – say it was mine alone! But what I still can't understand is how women can so quickly match their mood and appearance to the circumstances. You were flushed, you were crying, you seemed embarrassed . . . To be honest, you still do!

COUNTESS (*forcing herself to smile*). Yes, I was flushed . . . with anger at your suspicions. But it seems men aren't subtle enough to distinguish between righteous indignation, when an honest soul has been insulted, and guilty confusion, when the charge is merited.

COUNT (*smiling*). And this page – improperly dressed, no coat on, practically naked . . .

COUNTESS (*pointing to* SUZANNE). You see him standing before you. Aren't you pleased it was her you found, and not the other? As a general rule, you're not exactly averse to meeting this one.

COUNT (*laughs out loud*). And all that pleading, those fake tears . . .

COUNTESS. You're making me laugh, but I don't feel like laughing.

COUNT. We think we know a thing or two about politics, and we're like babes in arms. It's you the King should be sending to London, Madame, you should be his ambassador! You women have obviously studied long and hard how to conceal your feelings, to do it so successfully!

COUNTESS. It's you men that drive us to it.

SUZANNE. Release us like prisoners on parole, sir, and you'll soon see if we can be trusted.

COUNTESS. Let's leave it at that, my Lord. I've perhaps gone too far, but my tolerance over so serious a matter ought at least to assure me of yours.

COUNT. Will you say again that you forgive me?

COUNTESS. Did I say that, Suzanne?

SUZANNE. I didn't hear it, ma'am.

COUNT. Well, say the word now!

COUNTESS. You think you deserve it, ungrateful wretch?

COUNT. For my repentance, yes.

SUZANNE. Honestly, to suspect Her Ladyship of having a man in her dressing-room!

COUNT. Yes, well, I've been severely punished for it!

SUZANNE. And to doubt her word when she tells you it's her maid!

COUNT. Rosine, are you really so unforgiving?

COUNTESS. Oh, Suzanne, how weak I am! What an example I'm setting you! (*Holds out her hand to the* COUNT.) No-one will ever believe in a woman's anger again.

SUZANNE. Ah, well – isn't this what it always comes down to with men, ma'am?

The COUNT *kisses his wife's hand passionately. Enter* FIGARO, *out of breath.*

FIGARO. Someone said Her Ladyship was unwell. I've come as quickly as I could . . . and I'm delighted to see it's nothing.

COUNT (*drily*). You're extremely solicitous.

FIGARO. As is my duty, sir. Anyway, since there appears to be nothing amiss, may I say that all Your Lordship's young people, men and women both, are waiting downstairs with fiddles and bagpipes, ready to form an escort as soon as you give me permission to lead out my bride . . .

COUNT. And who's going to stay and look after the Countess?

FIGARO. Look after her? She's not ill, is she?

COUNT. No, but what about this mysterious man who's planning to meet her?

FIGARO. What mysterious man?

COUNT. The one in the letter you gave to Bazile!

FIGARO. Who told you that?

COUNT. If I didn't know it from another source, you villain, your own face would give you away, and prove you were lying.

FIGARO. Well, if that's the case, it's my face that's lying, not me.

SUZANNE. The game's up, Figaro dear, don't waste your breath. We've told him everything.

FIGARO. Told him what? You're treating me like another Bazile!

SUZANNE. We told him how you wrote that letter, so that when His Lordship came in he would believe that the young page was in the dressing-room, where I'd locked myself in.

COUNT. Now, what have you to say to that?

COUNTESS. There's no point in concealing anything now, Figaro – the joke's over.

FIGARO (*trying to fathom what's going on*). The joke's over, you say?

COUNT. Yes, played out. Unless you've anything to add?

FIGARO. Me? I just wish I could say the same for my wedding ceremony. So, if you wouldn't mind giving the order . . .

COUNT. You admit the business about the letter, then?

FIGARO. Since that's what Her Ladyship wants, and what Suzanne and you yourself want, then I suppose I'd better want it too. But to tell you the truth, sir, if I were in your place I wouldn't believe a word of it.

COUNT. Still lying, despite all the evidence! I'll end up getting very annoyed.

COUNTESS (*laughing*). Ah, the poor man! Why do you want him to tell the truth for once, sir?

FIGARO (*aside, to* SUZANNE). I warned him of the danger he was in. It's the least an honest man could do.

SUZANNE (*aside*). Have you seen the young page?

FIGARO (*aside*). He's still a bit shaken.

SUZANNE (*aside*). The poor dear.

COUNTESS. Come, sir – they're desperate to be married. It's only natural they're impatient. Let's go down for the ceremony.

COUNT (*aside*). And Marceline, Marceline . . . (*Aloud.*) I'd like to get changed, at least.

COUNTESS. What, for our own servants? I haven't, have I.

Enter ANTONIO, *slightly tipsy, carrying a pot of crushed wallflowers.*

ANTONIO. My Lord! My Lord!

COUNT. What is it, Antonio?

ANTONIO. Sir, you've got to put bars on the windows overlooking my flower-beds. People fling all sorts of things out of these windows – somebody's even just chucked a man out!

COUNT. From this window?

ANTONIO. Look at the mess they've made of my wallflowers!

SUZANNE (*aside, to* FIGARO). Watch out, Figaro! Watch out!

FIGARO. Sir, he's been drunk since this morning.

ANTONIO. No, you're wrong there. It's a hangover from yesterday, that's all. You see how people jump to conclusions?

COUNT (*incensed*). So, this man! Where is he?

ANTONIO. Where is he?

COUNT. Yes.

ANTONIO. That's what I'm saying, sir. I'd just like to get my hands on him. I mean, I'm your servant, sir – it's me that looks after the garden, all on my own, sir. And if some man falls into it, well, you understand – it's my reputation that's at stake.

SUZANNE (*aside, to* FIGARO). Change the subject, quickly!

FIGARO. So you're still drinking, are you?

ANTONIO. I'd go mad if I didn't.

COUNTESS. But to drink to excess like that . . .

ANTONIO. Drinking when we don't need to, and making love when we feel like it, ma'am – that's the only thing that sets us apart from the beasts.

COUNT (*heatedly*). Answer my question, or I'll have you sacked.

ANTONIO. And d'you think I'd go, sir?

COUNT. What do you mean?

ANTONIO (*tapping his forehead*). Well, if you haven't enough up here to hang onto a good servant, sir, I'm not so daft as to sack a good master.

COUNT (*shaking him in a rage*). You said someone threw a man out of this window?

ANTONIO. That's right, Excellency – just now it was – wearing a white shirt, and he upped and ran off, dammit, like a . . .

COUNT (*impatient*). Then what?

ANTONIO. Well, I'd have run after, but I'd given myself such a whack on the hand against the gate, that I couldn't move a muscle – on this finger here, see. (*Holding up his finger.*)

COUNT. But you'd recognise this fellow again?

ANTONIO. Oh, indeed I would, sir . . . if I'd got a good look at him!

SUZANNE (*aside, to* FIGARO). He didn't see him.

FIGARO. All this fuss about a flower-pot! How much do you want for your wallflowers, you old misery? Sir, there's no point in searching – it was me that jumped out.

COUNT. What d'you mean, it was you?

ANTONIO. 'How much do you want, you old misery?' Well, you've put on a bit of weight since then. You were a good deal shorter and slimmer when I saw you!

FIGARO. Well, naturally – you go into a crouch when you jump . . .

ANTONIO. No, I reckon it was more like what's-his-name . . . that skinny little page.

COUNT. Chérubin, you mean?

FIGARO. Oh, yes – with his horse too, no doubt, come back on purpose all the way from Seville, where he presumably is by now.

ANTONIO. I didn't say that – that's not what I said. I didn't see any horse jumping out, or I'd have said so.

COUNT. God give me strength!

FIGARO. Sir, I was in the maids' room, in a white shirt – it *is* extremely hot! . . . Anyway, I was waiting there for Suzanne, when I suddenly heard your Lordship's voice, and a terrible racket going on. And I don't know what came over me, but I took fright because of that letter. It was stupid of me, I must admit, but I jumped out onto the flower-beds without thinking – I even sprained my ankle slightly. (*Rubs his foot.*)

ANTONIO. Well, if it was you, I suppose I'd better give you this scrap of paper that dropped out of your coat when you fell.

COUNT (*seizing it*). Give it to me! (*He looks at the paper, then folds it up again.*)

FIGARO (*aside*). I've had it now.

COUNT (*to* FIGARO). I dare say your terror won't have made you forget what was written on this paper, or how it came to be in your pocket?

FIGARO (*embarrassed, rummages through his pockets and pulls out various papers*). Of course not . . . It's just that I've so many. And I've got to reply to them all . . . (*Looks at one piece of paper.*) What's this? Oh, yes – it's a letter from Marceline – four pages, very nice . . . And this one – could be the petition from that poor man – that poacher, who's in jail now. Ah, no – this is it . . . And I had the inventory of the palace furniture in my other pocket . . . (*The* COUNT *unfolds the paper he is holding.*)

COUNTESS (*aside, to* SUZANNE). Oh, my God, Suzanne – it's his officer's commission!

SUZANNE (*aside, to* FIGARO). The game's up – it's Chérubin's commission!

COUNT (*folds the paper up again*). Well, well, Mr Clever, can't you guess?

ANTONIO (*goes up to* FIGARO). His Lordship says, can't you guess?

FIGARO (*pushes him away*). Stand back, you old goat – don't breathe on me!

COUNT. So, you can't remember what it was?

FIGARO. Ah! Oh, dear! Oh, dear! That must be the poor boy's commission – he gave it to me, and I forgot to return it. Oh, God, how silly of me! What's he going to do without his commission? I'll have to run and . . .

COUNT. Why would he give it to you?

FIGARO (*embarrassed*). He . . . er . . . he wanted me to do something to it.

COUNT (*examines the paper*). There's nothing the matter with it.

COUNTESS (*aside, to* SUZANNE). The seal.

SUZANNE (*aside, to* FIGARO). The seal's missing.

COUNT (*to* FIGARO). You're not answering.

FIGARO. Actually, it's . . . er . . . there's something missing. He said it was the custom to . . .

COUNT. Custom? What custom? The custom to what?

FIGARO. To seal it. To fix your coat of arms to it. Of course, maybe it wasn't worth the trouble.

COUNT (*Looks at the paper again and screws it up in a rage*). Damn! I'm obviously fated to know nothing! (*Aside.*) It's Figaro that's at the bottom of this – by God, I'll have my revenge! (*Makes to exit in high dudgeon.* FIGARO *stops him.*)

FIGARO. You're leaving without authorising my wedding?

Enter MARCELINE, BAZILE, *various servants and tenants of the* COUNT.

MARCELINE. Don't permit it, sir! Before you grant him any favours, you must see justice done between us. He has certain obligations to me.

COUNT (*aside*). Now's my chance for revenge!

FIGARO. Obligations? What obligations? Explain yourself.

MARCELINE. Oh, I'll explain myself all right, you villain! (*The* COUNTESS *sits down on a settee.* SUZANNE *stands behind her.*)

COUNT. What's this all about, Marceline?

MARCELINE. A promise of marriage.

FIGARO. No, a receipt for money she lent me, nothing more.

MARCELINE (*to the* COUNT). On condition he would marry me. Sir, you're a great nobleman, the chief magistrate of the province . . .

COUNT. Bring your case before the district court – that's where I dispense justice to all and sundry.

BAZILE (*pointing to* MARCELINE). In that case, Your Lordship will perhaps allow me to press my claims on Marceline too?

COUNT (*aside*). Aha! This is the wretch with the letter!

FIGARO. Another madman of the same type!

COUNT (*angrily, to* BAZILE). Your claims, your claims! You've a cheek to open your mouth here, you prize idiot!

ANTONIO (*clapping his hands*). Got him in one, by God! That's him all right!

COUNT. Marceline, we'll postpone the wedding until your claims have been considered, which will take place publicly in the Great Hall. Honest Bazile, my good and faithful servant – you can go into town now and find the members of the council.

BAZILE. For her case?

COUNT. And you can also bring me the peasant who delivered the letter.

BAZILE. Am I supposed to know him?

COUNT. You object?

BAZILE. Well, I didn't come to the castle to run errands.

COUNT. What for, then?

BAZILE. To exercise my talent, sir – I am the local
  organist, I give harpsichord lessons to Her Ladyship,
  I teach singing to her ladies, and the mandolin to her
  pages, but I am chiefly employed to entertain Your
  Lordship's guests with my guitar, when it pleases you to
  command me.

GRIPE-SOLEIL (*steps forward*). Sir, I'll go, if you like.

COUNT. What's your name and what do you do?

GRIPE-SOLEIL. Gripe-Soleil's my name, Your Honour – I
  look after the goats, I do, and I've been called down here
  for the fireworks. So I'm having a holiday from the goats,
  like, and I know where to find all them crazy lawyers.

COUNT. I'm impressed by your enthusiasm – off you go,
  then. As for you, sir – (*To* BAZILE.) You can accompany
  this gentleman with your guitar, and sing to keep him
  entertained on the road. He's one of my guests.

GRIPE-SOLEIL (*delighted*). What, me? A guest? (SUZANNE
  motions him to be quiet, pointing out the COUNTESS.)

BAZILE (*astonished*). What, I've to go with Gripe-Soleil and
  play for him? . . .

COUNT. It's your job, isn't it. Now go, or you're sacked.
  (*Exits.*)

BAZILE (*to himself*). Well, there's no point in arguing with
  the big fish, when I'm only . . .

FIGARO (*aside*). A minnow.

BAZILE (*aside*). Anyway, instead of joining their wedding
  celebrations, I'll go off and attend to my own with
  Marceline. (*To* FIGARO). Don't settle anything till I get

back, right? (*He goes to collect his guitar from the armchair upstage.*)

FIGARO (*follows him*). Don't settle anything? Oh, go on, clear off – I don't care if you never come back. You don't seem in the mood for singing – d'you want me to start you off? Come on, cheer up – let's have a doh-re-mi for my fiancée!

Begins walking backwards, dancing and singing a 'seguidilla'. BAZILE accompanies him, and everyone joins in the procession.

What care I for treasure?
My pleasure
Is my Suzanne,
Suzanne, Suzanne!
Suzanne, Suzanne,
Suzanne!

So sweet and kind,
Forever mine,
And I'm her man –
Suzanne, Suzanne!
Suzanne, Suzanne,
Suzanne!

The sound fades away as they dance out.

COUNTESS (*seated in her easy-chair*). Well, Suzanne, you see the mess that silly man of yours has got me into with that letter.

SUZANNE. Oh, ma'am, if you could have seen your face when I came back out of the dressing-room! It went white as a sheet, but that was just a passing cloud, as it were – then bit by bit you turned bright red!

COUNTESS. So he actually jumped out of the window?

SUZANNE. Without a moment's hesitation, the sweet boy! Floated out, like a butterfly!

COUNTESS. Oh, and that wretched gardener! That whole business left me so shaken I couldn't string two ideas together.

SUZANNE. On the contrary, ma'am – that just made me realise how moving in the best circles teaches a lady how to lie without batting an eyelid.

COUNTESS. Do you think we fooled the Count? What if he finds Chérubin's still in the castle?

SUZANNE. I'll tell him to keep so well hidden that . . .

COUNTESS. He'll have to leave. After all that's happened, you can well imagine I'm not keen on sending him to take your place in the garden.

SUZANNE. Well, I'm certainly not going. So there goes my wedding again . . .

COUNTESS (*stands up*). Hold on . . . Instead of sending you, or someone else, what if I were to go myself?

SUZANNE. You, ma'am?

COUNTESS. No-one need run any risk . . . And the Count wouldn't be able to deny it . . . To punish him for his jealousy, and prove his infidelity, would be . . . Yes, come on – we've had one stroke of luck already, I feel like trying for a second. Let him know right away that you'll meet him in the garden. But make sure no-one else . . .

SUZANNE. What about Figaro?

COUNTESS. No, no! He'd only want to interfere . . . Bring me my mask and cane – I'll go out onto the terrace and think about it. (SUZANNE *goes into the dressing-room.*) It's really rather daring, this little scheme of mine. (*Turns round.*) Ah! My ribbon! My pretty little ribbon – I'd almost forgotten you! (*Retrieves it from the easy-chair and rolls it up.*) I'm never going to part with you – you'll always remind me of the scene when that unhappy boy . . . Ah! My Lord, what have you done? And what about me? What am I doing now?

SUZANNE *re-enters. The* COUNTESS *slips the ribbon furtively into her bosom.*

SUZANNE. Your cane and mask, ma'am.

COUNTESS. Now, remember – not one word about this to Figaro.

SUZANNE (*delightedly*). Ma'am, it's a brilliant scheme! I've just been thinking about it. It draws all the strands together, and ties everything up so neatly. And no matter what happens, my wedding's guaranteed now. (*She kisses the* COUNTESS' *hand, and they exit.*)

During the act interval, servants prepare the Great Hall. Two high-backed benches are brought on for the lawyers, and placed at either side of the stage, leaving a passage free at the rear. A platform with two steps is positioned upstage centre, and the COUNT's *chair placed on it. The clerk's table and stool are set downstage, and there are seats for* BRID'OISON *and the other judges on either side of the* COUNT.

ACT THREE

The scene is a room in the castle, known as the Throne Room, and serving as an audience chamber; on one side there is a dais, with a canopy over a portrait of the King.

Enter the COUNT *and* PÉDRILLE, *wearing a jacket and riding-boots, and holding a sealed packet.*

COUNT (*brusquely*). You're sure you understand?

PÉDRILLE. Yes, Your Excellency. (*Exits.*)

COUNT (*calling after him*). Pédrille!

PÉDRILLE (*returns*). Excellency?

COUNT. No-one saw you?

PÉDRILLE. Not a living soul.

COUNT. Take the Arab.

PÉDRILLE. He's at the gate, saddled and ready.

COUNT. Good! Ride straight to Seville, then.

PÉDRILLE. It's only twenty miles, sir, that's easy.

COUNT. When you get there, find out if the page has arrived yet.

PÉDRILLE. At the house?

COUNT. Yes – and how long he's been there, in particular.

PÉDRILLE. I understand, sir.

COUNT. Hand over his commission, and come back immediately.

PÉDRILLE. And supposing he isn't there?

COUNT. Then come back even quicker, and give me the whole story. Now go!

Exit PÉDRILLE.

I've done a really stupid thing, getting rid of Bazile. My bad temper'll be the ruin of me. That note he sent, warning me of a plot against the Countess – that business of the maid locked in the dressing-room when I arrived . . . her mistress in a state of terror, whether real or feigned . . . a man who jumps out of the window, then someone who confesses, or pretends it was him . . . I can't make head or tail of it. There's something mysterious going on here. And servants taking liberties like that – well, it's of no consequence when it's that sort of people. But the Countess! If some impudent creature were to try and . . . No, no, I'm getting carried away. The truth is, when you lose your temper, even the best regulated imagination can run mad! She was having some fun, that's all – trying not to laugh, that ill-concealed delight. She has some self-respect, surely. And then there's my honour . . . yes, how the devil does that stand? On the other hand, what about me? Has that little baggage Suzanne given away my secret? Anyway, she's not married to him yet, is she. So how have I managed to get entangled in all this nonsense? I've tried to give it up a dozen times . . . Indecisiveness, that's my trouble! If I was absolutely sure I wanted her, I'd have scarcely any desire for her. Oh, this Figaro knows how to keep a person waiting! I'll sound him out carefully . . .

(FIGARO *appears upstage – pauses*.) and try to discover, in the course of the conversation, in a sort of roundabout way, whether he knows about my feelings for Suzanne.

FIGARO (*aside*). Here we go.

COUNT. . . . If she's said one word to him . . .

FIGARO (*aside*). He suspects me, I fear.

COUNT. . . . I'll make him marry the old woman.

FIGARO (*aside*). What, Bazile's beloved?

COUNT. . . . Then we'll see what we can do with the young one.

FIGARO (*aside*). My wife, if you please!

COUNT (*turning round*). Eh? What? What was that?

FIGARO (*coming forward*). It's me – you sent for me.

COUNT. And what made you say that?

FIGARO. I didn't say anything.

COUNT. 'My wife, if you please . . . '

FIGARO. It was . . . er, I was talking to somebody: 'Go and tell my wife, if you please'.

COUNT (*begins pacing up and down*). His *wife!* . . . And might I ask what business can detain you, sir, when I've called for you?

FIGARO (*pretending to adjust his clothes*). I got dirty falling into the flower-beds, so I had to change.

COUNT. And that takes an hour?

FIGARO. It does take time.

COUNT. Hm, the servants in this house spend longer getting dressed than their masters!

FIGARO. Well, they don't have valets to assist them.

COUNT. I still don't understand what possessed you to take such a stupid risk, flinging yourself out of . . .

FIGARO. Risk? Good heavens, you'd think I'd been buried alive . . .

COUNT. Don't play the innocent with me, you crafty devil! You know perfectly well I'm not concerned about the risk, it's your motive that bothers me.

FIGARO. Well, you arrive on a false premise, absolutely raging, turning everything upside down, like some sort of mountain torrent – you're looking for a man, and by God you'll have him, if you've got to break down the doors, force open the locks. I just happened to be there, by sheer chance, and well, the state you were in, sir, who knows what . . .

COUNT (*cutting him off*). You could have got out by the stairs.

FIGARO. Yes, and let you catch me in the corridor?

COUNT (*angrily*). In the corridor! (*Aside.*) I'm losing my temper, and I won't find out what I need to know.

FIGARO (*aside*). He's getting warm – we'll have to box cleverly.

COUNT (*calmed down again*). Anyway, that's not what I wanted to talk about – we'll forget that. I'd had an idea . . . yes, I'd been thinking of taking you with me to London, as my courier, but on reflection . . .

FIGARO. Your Lordship has changed his mind?

COUNT. Well, in the first place, you don't know any English.

FIGARO. I know 'God damn!'

COUNT. I don't understand.

FIGARO. I said, I know 'God damn!'

COUNT. So?

FIGARO. Eh? Why, English is a damnably fine language! You can make a little go such a long way. With a good 'God damn!' in England, you need never be stuck for anything. You fancy a nice plump chicken? Just go into a tavern and do like so to the waiter (*Mimes turning a spit.*) 'God damn!' He'll bring you a hunk of salt beef, without bread. It's quite remarkable. You feel like a glass of excellent burgundy or claret? All you do is this . . . (*Mimes uncorking a bottle.*) 'God damn!' He'll bring you a foaming tankard of beer, in best pewter. Wonderfully satisfying! Or let's say you run into one of these sweet young things tripping along, her eyes modestly lowered, her elbows tucked in, her hips gently swaying – and you give her an affectionate pat on the cheek . . . Ah! 'God damn!' She'll give you one right between the eyes, just to prove she understands you. True enough, the English drop in a few other words here and there in conversation, but it's perfectly clear that 'God damn!' is the basis of the language. So, if Your Lordship has no other reason for leaving me in Spain . . .

COUNT (*aside*). He wants to come to London. She can't have said anything.

FIGARO (*aside*). He thinks I know nothing. Let's keep him
    in that frame of mind for a while.

COUNT. What reason had the Countess for playing such a
    trick on me?

FIGARO. To be frank, My Lord, you know far better than I.

COUNT. I anticipate her every desire, I shower her with
    presents . . .

FIGARO. You give her things, yes, but you're unfaithful to
    her. Are we grateful for the little extras to someone who
    deprives us of the necessities?

COUNT. You know, there was a time when you used to tell
    me everything.

FIGARO. And I'm concealing nothing from you now.

COUNT. How much did the Countess give you for your
    part in this little scheme?

FIGARO. How much did you give me for prising her out of
    the Doctor's clutches? Come, sir, let's not humiliate the
    man who does us good service, or you'll make a bad
    valet out of him.

COUNT. Why is there always something cock-eyed about
    everything you do?

FIGARO. Because that's how you see everything, trying to
    find faults.

COUNT. You have a hateful reputation!

FIGARO. And supposing I deserve better? Are there many
    gentlemen who could say the same?

COUNT. I've seen you a hundred times on the road to
    fortune, and you never get there.

FIGARO. What do you expect? It's jam-packed, everyone's running like mad, shoving and pushing, elbowing each other out of the way, knocking each other down, to get there first, and to hell with the rest! That's how it is, and as far as I'm concerned you can keep it.

COUNT. What, your fortune? (*Aside.*) That's news.

FIGARO (*aside*). Now it's my turn. (*Aloud.*) Your Excellency was kind enough to appoint me steward of the castle. That's an extremely pleasant job. True, I shan't now be the bearer of all sorts of interesting news, but on the other hand, living contentedly with my wife in the heart of Andalusia . . .

COUNT. What's to prevent you taking her with you to London?

FIGARO. I'd have to leave her so often I'd soon get fed up with marriage.

COUNT. You know, with your brains and character you could go far in the service.

FIGARO. Go far with brains? Your Lordship's making fun of me. Mediocrity and the ability to crawl, that'll get you anywhere.

COUNT. All you need is a little study of the political scene, under my direction.

FIGARO. I know it already.

COUNT. What, like English? The basis of the language?

FIGARO. Yes, not that it's anything to brag about. To feign ignorance of what one knows, and knowledge of what one doesn't; to hear things one doesn't understand, and be quite deaf to what one hears; above all to overstretch one's abilities; to make a great secret out of hiding what doesn't exist; to shut oneself away, for the purpose of sharpening pencils; to give an impression of profundity, when one is in fact, as they say, an empty vessel; to act out a part, either well or badly; to deploy spies and reward traitors; to intercept and unseal private letters; to attempt to gloss over the poverty of one's means, by exaggerating the importance of one's ends – and there you have it, that's politics, or I'm a Dutchman.

COUNT. Ah, but that's intrigue you're describing.

FIGARO. Politics, intrigue – have it your way. They're pretty much the same, whichever way you look at them. But as the old song goes: "I'd rather have my darling girl!"

COUNT (*aside*). He wants to stay here. I see now . . . Suzanne has betrayed me.

FIGARO (*aside*). I'll trick him, and pay him back in his own coin.

COUNT. So, you expect to win your case against Marceline?

FIGARO. Would you make it a crime for me to refuse an old maid, when Your Excellency permits himself to rob us of all the young ones?

COUNT (*mockingly*). In court the magistrate sets aside his own interests, and sees nothing but the law.

FIGARO. Which is easy on the rich, and tough on the poor . . .

COUNT. Do you think I'm joking?

FIGARO. Ah! Who knows, My Lord? *Tempo è galant'uomo*, as the Italians say – time will tell. We'll soon find out who means us harm and who doesn't.

COUNT (*aside*). He's obviously been told everything. Well, he'll marry the old lady.

FIGARO (*aside*). He's been testing me. How much does he know?

Enter a LACKEY.

LACKEY (*announcing*). Don Gusman Brid'oisin.

COUNT. Brid'oisin?

FIGARO. Ah yes, of course. The judge, your companion on the bench, and fellow-magistrate.

COUNT. Send him in. (*Exit the* LACKEY.)

FIGARO *stands for a moment or two observing the* COUNT, *who is deep in thought.*

FIGARO. Is there anything more Your Lordship requires?

COUNT. What? Oh yes – I'd like this room set out for the hearing.

FIGARO. Eh? What else is needed? The large armchair for you, some decent seats for your colleagues, a stool for the clerk, two benches for the lawyers, the floor for the gentry, and the rabble at the back. I'll go and dismiss the cleaners now. (*Exits.*)

COUNT. That crafty devil makes a fool of me! He's so quick to get on top in an argument, he backs you into a corner, ties you up in knots. They're scoundrels, the pair of them, out to take advantage of me. Well, you can be friends, lovers, whatever you like, I don't care, but husband and wife, never!

Enter SUZANNE, *out of breath.*

SUZANNE. My Lord . . . I beg your pardon, My Lord . . .

COUNT (*drily*). What is it, young lady?

SUZANNE. Oh, you're angry.

COUNT. I presume you're looking for something?

SUZANNE (*meekly*). It's my mistress, sir – she has the vapours. I've run up here to ask you to lend us your smelling-salts. I'll bring them back right away.

COUNT (*gives her the flask*). No, no, keep them yourself. You'll find a use for them soon enough.

SUZANNE. You don't seriously imagine women in my position have the vapours? It's an aristocratic malady – you can only catch it in boudoirs.

COUNT. Well, a young woman in love, about to lose her future husband . . .

SUZANNE. Ah, but if you pay off Marceline with the dowry money you've promised me . . .

COUNT. The dowry *I* promised?

SUZANNE (*lowering her eyes*). My Lord, I was sure I heard you.

COUNT. Yes, if only you *would* consent to hear me.

SUZANNE (*her eyes still lowered*). Isn't it my duty to listen to Your Excellency?

COUNT. What? So why didn't you say that before, cruel child?

SUZANNE. Is it ever too late to tell the truth?

COUNT. Then you'll be in the garden this evening?

SUZANNE. I walk there every evening, don't I?

COUNT. You know, you were very cold with me this morning.

SUZANNE. This morning? With the page hiding behind the chair?

COUNT. Yes, she's right. I'd forgotten that. But why this constant rejection, when Bazile, on my behalf, has already . . . ?

SUZANNE. What do we need a Bazile for?

COUNT. She's right, as always. However, there's a certain Figaro, and I fear you might have told him everything.

SUZANNE. Good heavens, of course I tell him everything . . . except what I have to keep quiet about.

COUNT (*laughing*). Charming! So, you promise? Now, let's be quite clear, dear heart – if you go back on your word . . . No rendezvous – no dowry, no marriage.

SUZANNE (*curtseying*). And no marriage, no *droit de seigneur*, My Lord.

COUNT. Where does she get all this? Honest to God, I'll run wild for her! Anyway, your mistress is waiting for her smelling-salts . . .

SUZANNE (*laughing, gives him back the flask*). How could I have spoken to you without an excuse?

COUNT (*tries to kiss her*). Delicious creature!

SUZANNE (*breaks free*). Someone's coming.

COUNT (*aside*). She's mine. (*Makes his escape.*)

SUZANNE. Now, let's hurry and tell Her Ladyship.

Enter FIGARO.

FIGARO. Suzanne, Suzanne! Where are you rushing off to, after leaving His Lordship . . . ?

SUZANNE. Go to court now, if you wish. You've just won your case! (*Quickly exits.*)

FIGARO (*following her*). Eh? Well, tell me, then . . . (*Exits.*)

The COUNT *re-enters.*

COUNT. 'You've just won your case'! Well, what a fine trap I was walking into! Oh, my insolent young friends, I'll make you suffer for this . . . Yes, that'll be a fitting judgement, right and proper . . . But supposing he were to pay the old woman? No . . . what's he going to pay with? Hah! Anyway, haven't I the proud Antonio? An arrogant old man – he absolutely despises Figaro. What, let some nobody marry his niece? So, I'll feed his obsession . . . yes, why not? In the vast field of intrigue one must learn to cultivate everything – even the vanity of an old fool. (*He calls out.*) Antonio! (*He sees* MARCELINE *and the others coming, and exits.*)

Enter BARTHOLO, MARCELINE *and* BRID'OISIN, *wearing his magistrate's gown.*

MARCELINE (*to* BRID'OISIN). Sir, please listen to my case.

BRID'OISIN (*with a slight stammer*). Very well. Let's discuss it verbally.

BARTHOLO. It's about a promise of marriage.

MARCELINE. Accompanied by a loan of money.

BRID'OISIN. I understand — the usual story, *et cetera*.

MARCELINE. No, sir, there's no *et cetera*.

BRID'OISIN. Ah, I see — you have the money.

MARCELINE. No, sir — I lent it to *him*.

BRID'OISIN. Ah, now I see — you're wanting it back?

MARCELINE. No, sir — I want him to marry me.

BRID'OISIN. Ah, of course, of course — I see now, yes. And does he want to marry you?

MARCELINE. No, sir, and that's what this case is all about!

BRID'OISIN. Yes, yes — do you think I don't understand that?

MARCELINE. No, sir. (*To* BARTHOLO.) Where are we? (*To* BRID'OISIN.) And you're going to be trying our case?

BRID'OISIN. Well, I didn't purchase this office to do anything else.

MARCELINE (*sighing*). It's nothing short of an abuse, selling such things!

BRID'OISIN. It is indeed. They'd do better to give us them for nothing. So, who are you suing?

FIGARO *re-enters, rubbing his hands.*

MARCELINE (*pointing to him*). That lying cheat there, sir.

FIGARO (*cheerfully, to* MARCELINE). I'm annoying you, perhaps? (*To* BRID'OISIN.) His Lordship will be here in a moment, sir.

BRID'OISIN. I've seen this fellow somewhere before.

FIGARO. At your good lady wife's, sir, in Seville – I was in her service.

BRID'OISIN. When was that?

FIGARO. A bit less than a year before the birth of your youngest son, sir – a fine handsome boy, if I may say so.

BRID'OISIN. Yes, he's the best-looking of the lot. So, I hear you're up to your old tricks again?

FIGARO. You're too kind, sir. This is a trivial matter.

BRID'OISIN. A promise of marriage. Ah, the silly boy!

FIGARO. Sir . . .

BRID'OISIN. Has this young man seen my secretary?

FIGARO. Isn't that Double-Main, the clerk of the court?

BRID'OISIN. That's right – he's got a finger in every pie.

FIGARO. A finger? Both hands, more like! Oh yes, I've already seen him about the plea, and the supplementary plea, and all the rest of the business.

BRID'OISIN. One must observe the proper forms.

FIGARO. Oh, for sure, sir – the case might start out with the litigants, but when it comes to court, the forms make a tidy little inheritance for the lawyers, we all know that.

BRID'OISIN. This young man isn't as simple as I first thought. Well then, my friend, since you know so much, we'll take good care of your interests.

FIGARO. Sir, I shall rely on your sense of justice, even though you are a judge.

BRID'OISIN. What? Yes, I am a judge. But if you owe money, and you won't pay it . . .

FIGARO. Then clearly, sir, it's as if I didn't owe a thing.

BRID'OISIN. Of course. Eh? What was that he said?

Enter the USHER, *preceding the* COUNT.

USHER. Gentlemen – His Lordship!

COUNT. In your judge's robes, Brid'oisin? This is a purely domestic affair. Ordinary clothes would have been good enough.

BRID'OISIN. As Your Lordship, indeed. However, I never act without them – it's the proper form, you see. A man may laugh at a judge in a jacket, who would tremble at the mere sight of a prosecutor in his gown. No no, we must observe the forms.

COUNT (*to the* USHER). You can admit the public.

USHER (*opens the doors, calling out*). Enter! Enter!

Enter ANTONIO, *with the castle* SERVANTS, *and* PEASANTS, *dressed for the occasion. The* COUNT *takes his seat in his great armchair,* BRID'OISIN *on a chair beside him; the* CLERK *sits on a stool at his table,* MAGISTRATES *and* LAWYERS *on benches;* MARCELINE *is at* BARTHOLO's *side;* FIGARO *on the other bench. The* PEASANTS *and* SERVANTS *stand at the rear.*

BRID'OISIN (*to* DOUBLE-MAIN). Double-Main, read out the cases.

DOUBLE-MAIN. (*reads out a document*). The noble, the extremely noble, the infinitely noble Don Pedro George, Hidalgo, Baron de los Altos, y Montes Fieros, y Otros

Montes, against one Alonzo Calderón, a young dramatic
author. It concerns a certain comedy, still-born, which
each disowns, and attributes to the other.

COUNT. They're both right. And the verdict of the court is
that if they collaborate on another piece, the nobleman
should supply his name, and the writer his talent.

DOUBLE-MAIN (*reads out another document*). André Petruccio,
labourer, against the Provincial Collector of Taxes – the
case concerns an unjust exaction . . .

COUNT. That's not within my remit. I'll serve my vassals
better by defending their interests at court. Next . . .

DOUBLE-MAIN (*picks up a third document. BARTHOLO and
FIGARO stand up*). Barbe – Agar – Madeleine – Nicole –
Marceline de Verte-Allure, spinster . . . (MARCELINE
rises and curtseys.) against Figaro . . . the Christian name's
left blank?

FIGARO. Anonymous.

BRID'OISIN. Anonymous? Which patron saint is that?

FIGARO. It's mine.

DOUBLE-MAIN (*writing*). Against Anonymous Figaro.
Status?

FIGARO. Gentleman.

COUNT. You're a gentleman? (*The CLERK writes it down.*)

FIGARO. Had it been God's will, I should have been the
son of a prince.

COUNT (*to the CLERK*). Carry on.

USHER (*calling out*). Silence in court!

DOUBLE-MAIN (*reads*). The case concerns an objection to the marriage of the aforesaid Figaro, lodged by the aforesaid Marceline de Verte-Allure. Doctor Bartholo will act on behalf of the plaintiff, and the aforesaid Figaro will plead his own cause, if the court will permit, contrary to the will and custom of this jurisdiction.

FIGARO. Custom, Master Double-Main, is often an abuse. With a little instruction, the client always understands his own case better than the kind of lawyers who rant and rave in a cold sweat, who know everything *except* their brief, and care as little about ruining their client, as they do about boring the court stiff, and sending the magistrates to sleep. They're more pompous and puffed-up than if they'd just delivered one of Cicero's Orations. Now, I'll put the case in a nutshell. My Lords . . .

DOUBLE-MAIN. That's a complete waste of time, since you're not the plaintiff. Your job is to defend yourself. Come forward, Doctor, and read out the promise of marriage.

FIGARO. Oh yes, the promise!

BARTHOLO (*putting on his spectacles*). It's set down very precisely.

BRID'OISIN. We'll have to see it.

DOUBLE-MAIN. Let's have some silence, gentlemen.

USHER (*calling out*). Silence in court!

BARTHOLO (*reads*). 'I, the undersigned, acknowledge having received from one Marceline de Verte-Allure, etc., in the castle at Aguas-Frescas, the sum of two thousand silver piastres, the which sum I shall repay to her on

demand at the said castle, and in consideration of which
I shall marry her, etc. Signed 'Figaro' – plain and simple.
My client's claim is for the repayment of her money, and
the fulfilment of that promise, with costs. (*He begins to
address the court.*) Gentlemen . . . Never has a more
intriguing case been submitted to the judgment of this
court! Not since Alexander the Great, who promised
marriage to the beautiful Thalestris . . .

COUNT (*interrupting*). Before we proceed, sir, are we agreed
on the validity of this document?

BRID'OISIN (*to* FIGARO). Have you any objections to the
paper as read?

FIGARO. I have, sirs – to the way in which it was read,
either through malice, error, or deliberate omission –
since it doesn't actually say: 'the which sum I shall repay,
and marry her', but 'the which sum I shall repay, *or*
marry her'. And that's an entirely different matter.

COUNT. Does it say 'and' in the document? Or is it
actually 'or'?

BARTHOLO. It's 'and'.

FIGARO. It's 'or'.

BRID'OISIN. Double-Main, you read it.

DOUBLE-MAIN (*taking the paper*). That's the safest way.
Parties to the case often deliberately misread it. (*He reads.*)
'Blah-blah-blah . . . Marceline . . . blah-blah-blah . . . de
Verte-Allure . . . Ah! 'The which sum I shall repay to her
on demand, at the said castle . . . *and* . . . *or* . . . *and* . . .
or . . . ' The word's so badly written . . . and there's a
blot.

BRID'OISIN. A what? Oh, a blot.

BARTHOLO (*to the court*). And I maintain, sirs, that it is the copulative conjunction 'and' which links the two subordinate clauses in this sentence, that is, I shall repay the lady, *and* I shall marry her.

FIGARO. And I maintain, sirs, that it is the alternative conjunction 'or' which separates the aforesaid clauses – that is, I shall repay the lady, *or* I shall marry her. And I'll out-pedant him. If he wants to talk Latin, I'll talk Greek and make mincemeat of him.

COUNT. How do we rule on a question like that?

BARTHOLO. Gentlemen, in order to cut the matter short, and not quibble over one word, we'll accept that it was 'or'.

FIGARO. I want that noted.

BARTHOLO. And we'll stick to it. The guilty party won't use that as a pathetic escape clause. Now, let us examine the document for another meaning. (*He reads.*) 'The which sum I shall repay to her at the said castle, where I shall marry her'. Gentlemen, that's like saying: 'You're going to be bled in this bed, where you'll stay and keep warm'. That is, this bed, *in which* . . . 'Take two grammes of rhubarb, wherein is to be mixed a little tamarind'. That is, *in which* is to be mixed . . . Accordingly, 'the said castle *where* I shall marry her', gentlemen, is 'the castle *in which* . . . '

FIGARO. Nothing of the sort. It says 'or', not 'where'. The meaning of the sentence is as follows: it'll be *either* the disease that kills you, *or* the doctor – that is, *or else* it'll be the doctor, there's no argument. Another example: *either* you'll write nothing worth reading, *or*, fools will decry you – that is, *or else* fools . . . the meaning's quite clear: *or*, knaves will slander you – that is, *or else* knaves – since in this case, fools or knaves are the governing substantive. Does Master Bartholo honestly think I've forgotten my grammar? Anyway, 'I shall repay her in the said castle, *comma*, or marry her' . . .

BARTHOLO (*hurriedly*). There's no comma.

FIGARO. Yes, there is. Gentlemen, it's *comma*, 'or else marry her'.

BARTHOLO (*glancing quickly at the paper*). There's no comma, sirs.

FIGARO. Well, there was one. Anyway, if a man marries, is he legally bound to repay his wife?

BARTHOLO. Yes. People keep their property separate when they marry.

FIGARO. And their bodies separate, if the marriage doesn't make them quits.

The MAGISTRATES *rise and discuss the matter in whispers.*

BARTHOLO. That's a funny way of calling quits!

DOUBLE-MAIN. Silence, gentlemen!

USHER (*calling out*). Silence in court!

BARTHOLO. And that's what this villain calls paying his debts!

FIGARO. Is this your case you're pleading, sir?

BARTHOLO. I'm defending this lady.

FIGARO. Then carry on raving, but leave out the insults. When the courts decided to allow third parties to plead cases, for fear the litigants would get carried away, they never intended that these calm defenders should become privileged slanderers. That's to demean a most noble institution. (*The* MAGISTRATES *continue their discussion in whispers.*)

ANTONIO (*to* MARCELINE, *indicating the* MAGISTRATES). What are they muttering about?

MARCELINE. Someone has bribed the judge, he's corrupting the others, and I'll lose my case.

BARTHOLO (*gloomily, under his breath*). That's what I'm afraid of.

FIGARO (*brightly*). Courage, Marceline!

DOUBLE-MAIN (*rises, and addresses* MARCELINE). Ha! That's going too far! I'm reporting you, and for the honour of this court, I demand that judgment be passed on this matter, before proceeding to the other.

COUNT (*sits down*). No, sir, I shall not pass judgment on the personal insult. A Spanish judge has no need to blush for excesses more fitting to an Asiatic court. There are plenty of other abuses. And I shall correct a second one of these, by giving you the reasons for my decision. Any judge who refuses to do so is a real enemy of the law. So, what can the plaintiff actually demand? Marriage in default of payment, yes. Both together would be incompatible.

DOUBLE-MAIN. Gentlemen, silence!

USHER (*calling out*). Silence in court!

COUNT. How does the defendant respond? If he wishes to retain his independence, he may do so.

FIGARO (*overjoyed*). I've won!

COUNT. However, since the document says: 'the which sum I shall repay on demand, or else marry,' etc., the court sentences the defendant to pay two thousand piastres to the plaintiff, or else marry her this very day. (*Rises.*)

FIGARO (*stunned*). I've lost!

ANTONIO (*delighted*). A splendid judgment!

FIGARO. What's splendid about it?

ANTONIO. That you're no longer going to be my nephew. Thank you very much, Your Lordship.

USHER (*calling out*). Clear the court! (*Exit the* PEOPLE.)

ANTONIO. I'll go and tell my niece. (*He exits.*)

The COUNT *is pacing up and down.*

MARCELINE (*sits down*). Ah! Now I can breathe again.

FIGARO. And I'm suffocating.

COUNT (*aside*). At least I've got my revenge, that's some consolation.

FIGARO (*aside*). And that Bazile, who was supposed to object to Marceline's marriage – when's he coming back? (*To the* COUNT, *about to exit.*) You're not leaving us, My Lord?

COUNT. The case is closed.

FIGARO (*to* BRID'OISIN). It's this great numskull of a lawyer . . .

BRID'OISIN. Numskull, me?

FIGARO. Absolutely. Anyway, I'm not going to marry her. I'm a gentleman, and that's that. (*The* COUNT *stops.*)

BARTHOLO. You will marry her.

FIGARO. What, without the consent of my noble parents?

BARTHOLO. Hah! What are their names? Show us them.

FIGARO. Just give me a little time. I'm very close to finding them. I've been searching for them the past fifteen years.

BARTHOLO. What an idiot! He's some foundling brat.

FIGARO. Not found, but lost, doctor – or rather stolen.

COUNT (*returning*). Stolen? Lost? Where's your proof? Now he'll complain he's being insulted.

FIGARO. My Lord, if the lace shawl and embroidered gown and gold bracelets, which the bandits found on me, didn't indicate my noble birth, then the care that was taken to give me some distinguishing marks would be proof enough that I was someone's beloved son. And this strange mark on my arm . . . (*Rolls up his sleeve.*)

MARCELINE (*leaping to her feet*). The mark of a spatula, on your right arm?

FIGARO. How do you know that?

MARCELINE. Oh, my God! It's him!

FIGARO. Yes, it's me.

BARTHOLO (*to* MARCELINE). And who's he?

MARCELINE (*agitated*). It's Emmanuel.

BARTHOLO (*to* FIGARO). You were kidnapped by gypsies?

FIGARO (*excitedly*). Yes, quite near a castle. Good doctor, if you can re-unite me with my noble family, you can name your own price. My illustrious parents wouldn't hesitate, they'd give heaps of gold.

BARTHOLO (*pointing to* MARCELINE). There is your mother.

FIGARO. My nurse?

BARTHOLO. Your true mother.

COUNT. His mother!

FIGARO. Explain yourself.

MARCELINE (*pointing to* BARTHOLO). And there is your father.

FIGARO (*anguished*). Oh! Oh, God help me!

MARCELINE. Hasn't nature told you so a thousand times?

FIGARO. No, never.

COUNT (*aside*). His mother!

BRID'OISIN. Well, it's obvious he won't marry her now.

BARTHOLO. Nor I.

MARCELINE. Nor you? What about your son? You gave me your sworn word . . .

BARTHOLO. I was mad. If every such relationship were binding, people would have to marry all sorts.

BRID'OISIN. Yes, and if we took a really close look, nobody would marry anybody.

BARTHOLO. It's the old old story – a misspent youth.

MARCELINE (*warming to her theme*). Misspent, oh yes, more than you'd think! I've no intention of denying my faults – they've been too well aired today! But it's hard having to atone for them now, after thirty years of modest living. I was a good person by nature, born so, and that's how I remained as long as I was allowed to use my reason. But at that age of illusions, of inexperience and urgent needs, when seducers lay siege to us and poverty thrusts its dagger into us, what can a mere child do against the assembled hordes of her enemies? The man who now judges us so severely has perhaps himself ruined a dozen such unfortunate women in his life!

FIGARO. Those most to blame are always the least forgiving – that's the way of things.

MARCELINE (*excitedly*). Yes, you ungrateful men, who condemn to scorn the playthings of your passion, your wretched victims – it's you who should be punished for the errors of our youth, you and your magistrates, so proud of their right to judge us, and who by their criminal negligence, deprive us of any honest means of making a living. Women have a natural right to make women's clothes, yet they train thousands of men to do the work.

FIGARO (*heatedly*). Yes, they even make soldiers learn embroidery!

MARCELINE (*getting carried away*). Even in the higher echelons of society, women are given no more than passing consideration – shown all the trappings of respect, apparently, but in fact kept in a state of servitude; treated like children when it comes to our worldly goods, but punished like adults for our faults! Ah! No matter how you look at it, your conduct towards us can only inspire horror, or pity!

FIGARO. She's right!

COUNT (*aside*). Too right!

BRID'OISIN. By God, she's right!

MARCELINE. But what does it matter to us, my son, that an unjust man denies us justice? Don't think about where you came from, but where you are going to. That's all that matters to any of us. In a few months your fiancée will be dependent on nobody; she'll accept you, I'll vouch for that. And from then on, you shall live with a wife, and a fond mother, who will vie with one another to see who can love you the most. Be gracious to them, my son, and enjoy your happiness. Be joyful, free, and generous with all the world, and your mother will ask for nothing more.

FIGARO. You speak most eloquently, mother, but I'll keep my own counsel. Honestly, what fools we are! This world's been turning now for thousands and thousands of years, and in all that vast ocean of time, out of which I've happened to snatch a paltry thirty years, gone for ever, never to return, I'm going to torture myself over who I owe them to? That's just too bad for people who worry about such things. Spending your life quibbling over that sort of stuff is just beating your head against a brick wall – it's like those wretched horses you see on a river tow-path, they never rest, they keep on pulling even after they've stopped moving. No, we'll take our chances.

COUNT. This absurd business is interfering with my plans!

BRID'OISIN (*to* FIGARO). And what about your noble birth, and the castle? You're playing tricks with the court, sir.

FIGARO. And this is a fine trick the court was going to make me play! The number of times I've been ready to beat this gentleman to death, over his wretched hundred crowns, and now it turns out he's my father! However, since Heaven has saved my virtue, and kept me from these dangers, please accept my apologies, father . . . and you, mother, embrace me . . . as maternally as you can manage. (MARCELINE *flings her arms round his neck.*)

SUZANNE *runs in, with a purse in her hand.*

SUZANNE. My Lord, stop! Don't let them marry! I can pay Madame now with the money my mistress has given me.

COUNT (*aside*). To hell with her mistress! It's as if they're all in this together . . . (*Exits.*)

ANTONIO (*to SUZANNE, catching sight of FIGARO embracing his mother*). Hold on, hold on! Don't pay yet!

SUZANNE (*turning away*). Right, I've seen enough. Let's get out of here, uncle.

FIGARO (*stopping her*). No, please! What is it you think you've seen?

SUZANNE. My stupidity, and your treachery.

FIGARO. Not more of one than the other.

SUZANNE (*angrily*). And you can damn well marry her, since you're so attached to her!

FIGARO (*cheerfully*). I'm attached to her, yes, but I'm not going to marry her. (SUZANNE *makes to exit, FIGARO holds her back.*)

SUZANNE (*slaps his face*). And you have the cheek to try and keep me here!

FIGARO (*to the others*). Now, what kind of love is that, eh? (*To* SUZANNE.) Before you leave us, I beg you, have a good look at this dear lady.

SUZANNE. I'm looking at her.

FIGARO. And? What do you think of her?

SUZANNE. She's horrible.

FIGARO. You see? Jealousy! Rears its ugly head again!

MARCELINE. My dear sweet Suzanne, come and give your mother a hug! This rascal who's teasing you is my son.

SUZANNE (*runs towards her*). You're his mother? (*They embrace.*)

ANTONIO. What, has this just come out now?

FIGARO. As far as I know.

MARCELINE (*excitedly*). No, no, my heart was drawn to him – it was only my reasons that were mistaken. It was the call of blood.

FIGARO. And it was my good sense, mother, that made me instinctively refuse you. I certainly didn't hate you – I mean, I did pledge the money . . .

MARCELINE (*hands him a piece of paper*). Here, it's yours. Our agreement – take it as your wedding gift.

SUZANNE (*flings the purse to him*). And take this too.

FIGARO. Thank you very much.

MARCELINE (*joyously*). From such a wretched life as a girl, I was about to become the most miserable of wives, and here I am now the most fortunate of mothers! Embrace

me, my two children! All my affections are united in you!
I'm as happy as I can possibly be! Oh, my dearest
children, I'm going to love you so much!

FIGARO (*touched, brightly*). Here, steady on, mother! Have a
care! D'you want to see me drowning my eyes with the
first tears I've ever known? Well, at least they're tears of
joy. You know, this is really stupid. I was almost ashamed
of them. I could feel them trickling down between my
fingers – look . . . (*Displays his fingers spread out.*) and like
an idiot, I was trying to hold them back! Begone, my
shame! I want to laugh and cry at the same time – you
don't have an experience like that twice. (*He embraces his
mother on one side, SUZANNE on the other.*)

MARCELINE. Oh, my boy!

SUZANNE. My dear boy!

BRID'OISIN (*wiping his eyes with a handkerchief*). Ah, well –
now I'm being silly too.

FIGARO (*excitedly*). Sorrow, I can defy you now! Touch me
if you dare, with these two dear women by my side!

ANTONIO (*to* FIGARO). That's enough lovey-doveying, if
you please. When two families marry, it's the parents who
go first, you know. Have yours joined hands yet?

BARTHOLO. Joined hands! Mine can wither and drop off
before I give it to the mother of such a fool!

ANTONIO (*to* BARTHOLO). So you're not his lawful
father, then? (*To* FIGARO.) In that case, my lad, there's
no point in going on.

SUZANNE. Oh, Uncle!

ANTONIO. What, d'you think I'm going to give my sister's child to somebody who's nobody's?

BRID'OISIN. You idiot, how can that be? Everybody's somebody's child.

ANTONIO. Fiddlesticks! He's not getting her – not ever! (*Exits.*)

BARTHOLO (*to* FIGARO). See if anyone'll adopt you.

He makes to exit, but MARCELINE *flings her arms round him and brings him back.*

MARCELINE. Stop, Doctor, don't go!

FIGARO (*aside*). I think every fool in Andalusia's out to wreck my marriage.

SUZANNE (*to* BARTHOLO). Dear kind father-in-law, he's your son!

MARCELINE (*to* BARTHOLO). In intelligence, ability, good looks!

FIGARO (*to* BARTHOLO). And he hasn't cost you a bean.

BARTHOLO. What about the hundred crowns he took off me?

MARCELINE (*caressing him*). We'll take such good care of you, papa!

SUZANNE (*caressing him*). We'll be so fond of you, dear little papa!

BARTHOLO (*touched*). Papa! Dear papa! Kind papa! Look at me, I'm even sillier than this gentleman! (*Indicating* BRID'OISIN.) I'm giving in like a child. (MARCELINE *and* SUZANNE *embrace him.*) No, no – I haven't said yes yet! (*Turns away.*) What's happened to His Lordship?

FIGARO. Let's run and catch him up – get his final word out of him. If he's gone off to plan some more trickery, we'll have to start all over again.

ALL. Let's go! Hurry! (*They drag* BARTHOLO *off with them.*)

BRID'OISIN. Well – 'sillier than this gentleman'! I could say a few things here myself, but . . . Hm . . . people round these parts aren't at all polite. (*Exits.*)

ACT FOUR

The scene is a gallery, decorated with candelabra, lighted chandeliers, flowers, garlands, etc., prepared for a celebration, in short. Downstage left is a writing-table with an armchair behind it.

FIGARO (*with his arm around* SUZANNE). Well now, my love, are you happy? That silver-tongued mother of mine has managed to persuade her Doctor. Like it or lump it, he's marrying her, and your villainous uncle's been silenced. The only one still fuming is His Lordship, because our marriage has now become the price of theirs. So go on, have a laugh at how splendidly it's all turned out.

SUZANNE. Have you ever seen anything so strange?

FIGARO. Or so funny. All we wanted was to squeeze a dowry out of His Excellency, and now we have two, nothing to do with him. You were being hunted by a ferocious rival, I was being tormented by a fury – that's all changed, and in her place we have the very best of mothers. Yesterday I was alone in the world, now I have both parents – not as grand, certainly, as I had imagined, loaded with titles and the like, but they'll do for us – we haven't the pretensions of the idle rich.

SUZANNE. Yet not one of the things you'd planned, and that we were waiting for, has actually happened!

FIGARO. Chance has done better than any of us, my dear. That's how it goes: you work, you scheme, you try to organise things one way, fate determines them in another. From the insatiable conqueror, out to gobble up the whole world, down to the harmless blind man with his dog, we're the playthings of the gods. And the blind man's often better led by his dog, frankly. He's less in the dark about what's in front of him, than the conqueror, that other blind creature, with all his hangers-on. As for that charming blind god we call Love . . . (*Takes her tenderly in his arms.*)

SUZANNE. That's the only one I'm interested in!

FIGARO. Then allow me to be the faithful dog that leads Love to your pretty little door, to dwell there forever.

SUZANNE. Love and you?

FIGARO. Me and Love.

SUZANNE. And you won't look for any other dwelling-place?

FIGARO. If you ever catch me at that, you can take a thousand million lovers and . . .

SUZANNE. You're protesting too much – tell me the truth.

FIGARO. My truth is the truest!

SUZANNE. What? You wretch, is there more than one sort?

FIGARO. Yes, of course there is. Ever since people first noticed how, with the passage of time, old follies become wisdom, and old white lies, planted without a thought, eventually grow into great truths, yes, there have been a thousand varieties. There are truths one knows, but dare not divulge, since not all truths can be freely uttered; there are truths one proclaims, without really believing, since not all truths are believable; there are lovers' vows, mothers' threats, drunken protestations, rich men's promises, shopkeepers' special offers – the list is endless. The only truth worth its salt is my love for Suzanne.

SUZANNE. I love it when you go on like that – it's silly, it shows you're happy. Now, let's talk about my rendezvous with the Count.

FIGARO. Let's not talk about it at all, ever. It almost cost me my Suzanne.

SUZANNE. So you don't want me to go?

FIGARO. Suzanne, if you really love me, then promise me this: that you'll let him cool his heels there on his own – it'll serve him right.

SUZANNE. It was a great deal harder for me to agree than it will be to break it off. So, that's that.

FIGARO. The truth?

SUZANNE. I'm not like you clever people – I only know one kind of truth.

FIGARO. And you will love me a little?

SUZANNE. A lot.

FIGARO. That's not much.

SUZANNE. What d'you mean?

FIGARO. When it comes to love, you know, even too much isn't enough.

SUZANNE. I don't understand all these subtleties, but I won't love anyone except my husband.

FIGARO. Keep your word, and you'll be a splendid exception to the rule. (*He makes to kiss her.*)

Enter the COUNTESS.

COUNTESS. Ah! I was right – wherever they are, I said, you can bet they'll be together. Now come along, Figaro, you're flying ahead of yourself, and your marriage, to steal a *tête-à-tête* now. People are waiting for you, and they're getting impatient.

FIGARO. That's true, ma'am, I'm forgetting myself. I'll go and show them my excuse. (*Exits, tries to take* SUZANNE *with him.*)

COUNTESS (*detaining her*). No, she'll follow in a moment. (*To* SUZANNE.) Now, have you everything you need for our change of clothes?

SUZANNE. We don't need anything, ma'am. The rendezvous is off.

COUNTESS. You've changed your mind?

SUZANNE. It's Figaro.

COUNTESS. You're tricking me.

SUZANNE. Good heavens, no!

COUNTESS. Figaro isn't the sort to pass up a handsome dowry.

SUZANNE. My Lady! What on earth do you mean?

COUNTESS. Just that now you've come to an agreement with the Count, you're sorry that you told me his plans. I can see what you're up to. Now leave me! (*Makes to exit.*)

SUZANNE (*falls to her knees*). In Heaven's name, ma'am, as we all hope to be saved – you don't know how you wrong me! After all your kindness, and the dowry you've given me . . .

COUNTESS (*lifting her up*). I'm sorry, my dear – I don't know what I'm saying. Look, if you let me take your place in the garden, you won't be there, so you'll keep your promise to your husband, and you'll help me to win mine back.

SUZANNE. You know, you really hurt me there.

COUNTESS. I was being stupid, that's all. (*Kisses her forehead.*) Where is the rendezvous to be?

SUZANNE (*kissing her hand*). The garden, that's all I can remember.

COUNTESS (*pointing to the table*). Take that pen and we'll arrange a meeting-place.

SUZANNE. Write to *him*?

COUNTESS. You'll have to.

SUZANNE. Ma'am, surely it's you who should . . .

COUNTESS. I'll take full responsibility. (SUZANNE *sits at the table, and the* COUNTESS *dictates.*) Now, that new song, how does it go? 'How wonderful this night will be, under the lovely chestnut tree . . . How wonderful this night will be . . . '

SUZANNE (*writing*). 'Under the lovely chestnut tree . . . ' What next?

COUNTESS. Do you think he won't understand?

SUZANNE (*re-reads it*). No, that's fine. (*Folds the note.*) What are we going to seal it with?

COUNTESS. Use a pin, and hurry! It'll serve for a reply. Write on the outside: 'Send back the seal'.

SUZANNE (*writes, laughing*). Ah! The seal. This is even funnier than the business of Chérubin's commission.

COUNTESS (*sighing at a painful memory*). Ah, yes.

SUZANNE (*after a search*). I haven't got a pin.

COUNTESS (*unfastening her dress*). Here, take this. (CHÉRUBIN's *ribbon falls to the floor*). Oh, my ribbon!

SUZANNE (*picks it up*). It's that little thief's. How could you be so cruel?

COUNTESS. I couldn't let him wear it on his sleeve, could I. That would've been really clever. Give it here.

SUZANNE. Your Ladyship isn't going to wear it now, stained with that young man's blood.

COUNTESS (*takes it back*). It'll do nicely for Fanchette. The first time she brings me flowers . . .

Enter a young shepherdess, CHÉRUBIN *in disguise,* FANCHETTE *and a number of young girls dressed likewise, carrying bouquets.*

FANCHETTE. My Lady, here are the girls from the village, bringing you flowers.

COUNTESS (*quickly hiding her ribbon*). Why, they're charming! I'm terribly sorry, my beautiful girls, that I don't know you all. (*Pointing to* CHÉRUBIN.) Who is this delightful child, who looks so modest?

SHEPHERDESS. She's a cousin of mine, ma'am – she's just come up for the wedding.

COUNTESS. She's very pretty. Well, since I can't carry twenty bouquets, let's do honour to the stranger. (*She takes the bouquet from* CHÉRUBIN *and kisses him on the forehead.*) Why, she's blushing! (*To* SUZANNE.) Suzanne, don't you think she looks like someone?

SUZANNE. The absolute image, ma'am, for sure.

CHÉRUBIN (*aside, hands on heart*). Oh! I've longed so much for that kiss!

Enter the COUNT *and* ANTONIO.

ANTONIO. I tell you he's here, My Lord. They got dressed in my daughter's room, and all his clothes are still there – see, here's his soldier's cap, which I took out of his pack.

He goes up and looks at all the girls, recognises CHÉRUBIN *and pulls off his woman's bonnet, so that his long military-style hair falls down. He then places the soldier's cap on* CHÉRUBIN'*s head.*

Well, well! Here's our officer!

COUNTESS (*draws back*). Oh, my God!

SUZANNE. The rascal!

ANTONIO. And it was him in Her Ladyship's room, I told you!

COUNT (*angrily*). Well, Madame?

COUNTESS. Sir, I'm more surprised than you are, and at least as annoyed!

COUNT. Yes, but what about this morning, then?

COUNTESS. I can't keep up the pretence any longer – that would be wrong of me. Yes, he had come to my room, and we set up the practical joke which these young people here have carried on. You came upon us by surprise while we were dressing him up, and you're so quick to react! Anyway, he took to his heels, and I was upset – the fright you gave us all did the rest.

COUNT (*testily, to* CHÉRUBIN). Why didn't you leave?

CHÉRUBIN (*hurriedly removing his cap*). My Lord . . .

COUNT. I shall punish your disobedience.

FANCHETTE (*innocently*). Oh, Your Lordship, listen to me! You know what you always say, whenever you come wanting to kiss me: 'If you'll just love me, my little Fanchette, I'll give you whatever you like'.

COUNT (*blushing*). Me? I said that?

FANCHETTE. Oh yes, Your Lordship! So instead of punishing Chérubin, give him to me in marriage, and I'll love you to distraction!

COUNT (*aside*). Bewitched by a page!

COUNTESS. Well, sir, it's your turn now. This child's confession, as innocent as my own, bears witness to two truths: that if I give you any cause for anxiety it's always unintentional, whereas you do everything in your power to add to mine, and to justify it, besides.

ANTONIO. What, you too, My Lord? Dammit, I'll have to set her to rights the way I did her late mother . . . It's of no consequence now, but Her Ladyship knows very well that when little girls grow up . . .

COUNT (*aside, disconcerted*). There's some evil genius at work here, turning everything against me!

Enter FIGARO.

FIGARO. My Lord, if you're going to detain our young ladies, we won't be able to start the festivities, or the dancing.

COUNT. Dancing? You? You shouldn't even consider it – not after that fall this morning, when you sprained your ankle.

FIGARO (*waggling his foot*). Well, I can still feel it, but it's nothing, really. (*To the young girls.*) Come along, my beauties, let's go!

COUNT (*detaining him*). You were very lucky that the flower-beds made such a soft landing.

FIGARO. Very lucky, undoubtedly. Otherwise . . .

ANTONIO (*detaining him*). Then again, he curled himself up into a ball as he fell.

FIGARO. Yes, a better jumper would've stayed in mid-air, wouldn't he. (*To the young girls.*) Are you coming, ladies?

ANTONIO (*detaining him again*). And all this time the little page was on his horse, galloping towards Seville, eh?

FIGARO. Galloping, or trotting, yes . . .

COUNT (*detaining him*). While you had his commission in your pocket?

FIGARO (*a little taken aback*). Yes, of course. Why all these questions? (*To the young girls.*) Now come along, girls, do!

ANTONIO (*catching hold of* CHÉRUBIN *by the arm*). And there's a girl here who can prove my future nephew is a liar.

FIGARO (*surprised*). Chérubin! (*Aside.*) A plague on the little fool!

ANTONIO. Are you with me?

FIGARO (*frantically*). Yes, yes, I'm with you . . . So, what yarn is he spinning?

COUNT (*coldly*). He's not spinning any yarn. He says that it was he who jumped onto the wallflowers.

FIGARO (*distracted*). Ah . . . Well, if he says so, it might've been. I'm not disputing something I know nothing about.

COUNT. So you're saying both of you . . .

FIGARO. Why not? Jumping's infectious – remember the Gadarene swine. And when Your Lordship's in a bad temper, anybody would prefer the risk . . .

COUNT. What, two at a time?

FIGARO. Two dozen, more like. Anyway, what does it matter – no-one was hurt. (*To the young girls.*) Now, are you coming or not?

COUNT (*irritated*). Is this some kind of comedy? (*A fanfare is heard off-stage.*)

FIGARO. Ah, that's the signal for the procession. To your places, my dears! Come, Suzanne, give me your arm. (*All rush off, leaving only* CHÉRUBIN, *his head bowed.*)

COUNT (*watching* FIGARO *go*). Well, if that isn't the height of impudence! (*To* CHÉRUBIN.) As for you, you sly creature, pretending to be ashamed of yourself – go and change your clothes immediately and keep out of my sight for the rest of the evening.

COUNTESS. He'll be extremely bored.

CHÉRUBIN (*innocently*). Bored? The happiness I'm wearing on my forehead now would be worth a hundred years in prison. (*He puts on his cap and rushes off.*)

The COUNTESS *stands speechless a few moments.*

COUNT. On his forehead? What's he so happy about?

COUNTESS (*embarrassed*). It's . . . it's his officer's cap, obviously. Everything's a toy to a child, after all. (*She makes to exit.*)

COUNT. Aren't you staying?

COUNTESS. You know I'm not feeling well.

COUNT. But you'll stay a moment for the sake of your maid, otherwise I'll think you're annoyed about something.

COUNTESS. Here come the two wedding parties – we'd better sit down to receive them.

COUNT (*aside*). Weddings! I suppose one must endure what one cannot prevent.

The COUNT *and* COUNTESS *sit down at one side of the stage. Enter the wedding parties to the tune of 'Les Folies d'Espagne', in march time. First come* HUNTSMEN, *shouldering their guns, then the* USHER, *the* MAGISTRATES *and* BRID'OISIN; *next,* PEASANTS *in their Sunday best, two* YOUNG GIRLS *carrying the bridal crown, two the white veil, and two the gloves and bouquet.* ANTONIO *gives his hand to* SUZANNE, *as the one who will give her away to* FIGARO. *More* YOUNG GIRLS *carry another bridal crown, veil and bouquet, like the first, for* MARCELINE. FIGARO *gives his hand to* MARCELINE, *as the one who will give her away to the* DOCTOR, *who brings up the rear with an enormous bouquet.*

The YOUNG GIRLS, *as they pass the* COUNT, *hand over the bridal regalia intended for* SUZANNE *and* MARCELINE *to his* VALETS. *The* PEASANTS *line up at opposite sides of the stage and begin dancing a fandango, with castanets. While the refrain is being played,* ANTONIO *leads* SUZANNE *up to the* COUNT, *and she kneels before him. The* COUNT *then places the bridal crown and veil on her head and hands her the bouquet, while two* YOUNG GIRLS *sing a duet:*

O, lovely bride, give praise and honour free –
Thy master doth renounce all claim on thee,
His pleasure doth forsake, his right abjure,
And leads thee to thy spouse a virgin pure!

SUZANNE *remains kneeling, and during the final couplet of the song she tugs at the* COUNT'*s coat and shows him her note; she then brings the hand nearest the audience up to her head and passes the note to the* COUNT *while he makes as if to adjust her bridal crown. He places it furtively inside his breast pocket; the singing comes to an end, and* SUZANNE *rises, making a deep curtsey.* FIGARO *comes forward to receive her from the* COUNT'*s hand, and withdraws with her to the opposite side of the stage, beside* MARCELINE, *while another fandango is being danced. The* COUNT *meanwhile, in haste to read* SUZANNE'*s note, goes towards the wings and pulls it out of his pocket, making the gesture of someone who has just been pricked by a pin. He waves his finger in the air, squeezes it, sucks it, then peers at the folded paper. N.B: During the following speeches, the orchestra plays very softly.*

COUNT. Damn these women, they stick pins in everything! (*He throws the pin away, reads the letter and kisses it, watched by* FIGARO.)

FIGARO (*to* SUZANNE *and* MARCELINE). It's obviously a love-letter, which some young woman has slipped him in passing. It's sealed with a pin, and it's had the effrontery to prick him.

The dancing is resumed, and the COUNT, *now having read the letter, turns it over and sees the invitation to reply by returning the pin. He searches for it on the floor, eventually retrieves it, and sticks it in his sleeve.*

FIGARO (*to* SUZANNE *and* MARCELINE). Everything's precious, when it comes from a loved one. Look, he's picked up the pin again. What a funny fellow he is!

SUZANNE is meanwhile exchanging signs with the COUNTESS. *The dance comes to an end, and the duet refrain begins.* FIGARO *now leads* MARCELINE *up to the* COUNT, *as* ANTONIO *had led* SUZANNE, *but just as the* COUNT *goes to take the bridal crown, and the duet is about to be sung, the proceedings are interrupted by cries off-stage.*

USHER (*at the door*). Stop, gentlemen, stop! You can't all come in here . . . Guards! Guards! (*The* GUARDS *move swiftly to the door.*)

COUNT (*rising*). What's going on?

USHER. My Lord, it's Don Bazile – he's got the whole village with him, and he's still singing!

COUNT. Let him come in, by himself.

COUNTESS. Please, may I be excused?

COUNT. I shan't forget your patience.

COUNTESS. Suzanne! . . . She'll come back. (*To* SUZANNE.) Let's go and change our clothes. (*She exits with* SUZANNE.)

MARCELINE. He always turns up at the wrong time.

FIGARO. Well, I'll make him sing to a different tune.

Enter BAZILE *with his guitar, and* GRIPE-SOLEIL.

BAZILE (*singing*). O, you faithful hearts and true,
Condemn not my philandering.
One love may be enough for you,
But let me go a-wandering!
The God of Love has wings to fly –
Tell me, then, why should not I?
The God of Love has wings to fly –
Tell me, then, why should not I?

FIGARO (*goes up to him*). Yes, that's exactly why he has
wings on his back. Now, my friend, what's all this racket
about?

BAZILE (*indicating* GRIPE-SOLEIL). Well, having proved
my loyalty to His Lordship by entertaining this
gentleman, His Lordship's guest, I believe, I might now
be able to demand justice for myself.

GRIPE-SOLEIL. Bah! He's not entertained me at all, Your
Lordship, nothing like – not with them mouldy old tunes.

COUNT. What is it you want, Bazile?

BAZILE. Only what belongs to me, Your Lordship – the
hand of Marceline, and I'm here to oppose . . .

FIGARO (*going closer to him*). Sir, how long since you last
looked a fool in the eye?

BAZILE. I'm doing that right now, sir.

FIGARO. Well, since my eyes obviously make a good
mirror for you, take this warning to heart. If you even
look like coming near this lady . . .

BARTHOLO (*laughing*). But why? Let's hear what he has to say.

BRID'OISIN (*stepping between them*). Now why should two friends . . .

FIGARO. Friends? Us?

BAZILE. Some hopes!

FIGARO. Because he writes boring hymn tunes?

BAZILE. And what about him? Nasty doggerel rhymes.

FIGARO. Street singer!

BAZILE. Scandal-sheet hack!

FIGARO. Oratorio squawker!

BAZILE. Diplomatic dogsbody!

COUNT (*seated*). One's as insolent as the other.

BAZILE. He insults me at every turn.

FIGARO. Whenever I get the chance, yes.

BAZILE. Telling everybody I'm nothing but a fool.

FIGARO. What do you take me for, an echo?

BAZILE. Yet there isn't a singer anywhere whose talent I haven't groomed.

FIGARO. Ruined, you mean.

BAZILE. You see, he's at it again!

FIGARO. Well, why not, if it's the truth? Are you some sort of prince, that you have to be buttered up? People have nothing to gain from lying to you, you old rogue, so you'll just have to put up with the truth. So if you're scared of hearing it from us, why are you trying to gatecrash our wedding?

BAZILE (*to* MARCELINE). Did you or did you not promise me that if you weren't spoken for within the next four years, you'd give me first refusal?

MARCELINE. Yes, but on what condition did I promise?

BAZILE. That if you were to find a certain lost child, I would adopt him.

ALL. He's found!

BAZILE. I don't believe it!

ALL (*pointing to* FIGARO). There he is!

BAZILE (*stepping back in alarm*). No, no, it's the Devil!

BRID'OISIN (*to* BAZILE). So . . . you renounce your claim to his dear mother?

BAZILE. What could be worse than having people think I was the father of a scoundrel?

FIGARO. Having them think you're the son of one. Are you getting at me?

BAZILE (*pointing at* FIGARO). Well, since this gentleman is obviously something here, for my part, I'd rather be nothing. (*Exits.*)

BARTHOLO. Ha ha ha ha!

FIGARO (*jumping for joy*). So I've finally got my wife!

COUNT (*aside*). And I my mistress! (*Rises.*)

BRID'OISIN (*to* MARCELINE). So everybody's happy.

COUNT. Have the two contracts drawn up. I'll sign them.

ALL. *Vive le Comte!* (*They exit.*)

COUNT. I need some peace and quiet. (*Makes to exit with the others.*)

GRIPE-SOLEIL (*to* FIGARO). And I'll go and set up the fireworks, under the big chestnut trees, as I was ordered.

COUNT (*turning back*). What? What fool gave that order?

FIGARO. What's wrong with that?

COUNT (*testily*). The Countess is feeling out of sorts. How is she going to see the display? You'll have to set it up on the terrace, facing her apartments.

FIGARO. You hear that, Gripe-Soleil? The terrace.

COUNT. Under the chestnut trees, the very idea! (*Aside, as he exits.*) They were going to light up my rendezvous!

FIGARO. Such tender regard for his wife! (*Makes to exit.*)

MARCELINE (*detains him*). A word, my son. I'd like to set things straight with you. A mistaken impression led me to do your charming wife an injustice – I thought she had some kind of arrangement with the Count, although according to Bazile, she'd always kept him at arm's length.

FIGARO. You don't know much about your son if you think he can be upset by these feminine impulses. I defy the cleverest of them to put one over on me.

MARCELINE. Well, it's a good thing you think like that, my son. Jealousy is . . .

FIGARO. . . . Nothing but the foolish offspring of pride, or the sickness of a fool. I've got my own views on that, mother . . . I couldn't care less, and if Suzanne should ever deceive me, well, I pardon her in advance. And she'll have to work at it . . . (*Turns round and catches sight of* FANCHETTE, *who seems to be looking for something.*) Ah! My dear little cousin is eavesdropping!

FANCHETTE. Oh no! That's not nice, everybody says so.

FIGARO. True enough. But it can be very useful, and they don't always say that.

FANCHETTE. I was looking to see if anyone was still here.

FIGARO. Telling lies already, you rascal! You know perfectly well he couldn't be.

FANCHETTE. Who?

FIGARO. Chérubin.

FANCHETTE. It's not him I'm looking for, I know perfectly well where he is. It's my cousin Suzanne.

FIGARO. And what does my little cousin want with her?

FANCHETTE. Well, since you're my cousin now, I'll tell you. It's . . . it's just a pin, I want to give it back to her.

FIGARO. A pin! A pin! And where did it come from, you brazen creature? Making a name for yourself at your age! (*Recovers his composure, then gently.*) You're doing a good job, Fanchette. It's most obliging of my little cousin . . .

FANCHETTE. So what are you so annoyed about? I'm going.

FIGARO (*detains her*). No no, I'm only teasing. Actually, this little pin of yours is the one His Lordship told you to give back to Suzanne – it was used to fasten a note he was holding. So you see, I know all about it.

FANCHETTE. Well, what are you asking me for, if you know so much?

FIGARO (*probing*). I just thought it would be amusing to find out how His Lordship came to make you his go-between.

FANCHETTE (*naively*). It's as you say: 'Here you are, little Fanchette – take this pin to your beautiful cousin, and just tell her it's the seal for the chestnut trees'.

FIGARO. For the what?

FANCHETTE. The chestnut trees. Oh, and he did say: 'Make sure nobody sees you'.

FIGARO. Well, you must do as you're told, cousin. Fortunately, nobody has seen you. So, run along and do your errand, and don't tell Suzanne any more than His Lordship has commanded.

FANCHETTE. Now why would I do that? He must take me for a fool, this cousin of mine. (*Exits skipping.*)

FIGARO. Well, mother?

MARCELINE. Well, son?

FIGARO (*almost choking*). Well, honest to God! Some things really are . . .

MARCELINE. Yes, they are indeed! Eh? What are they?

FIGARO (*clutching his chest*). It's something I've just heard, mother, and it's weighing me down here, like lead.

MARCELINE. So that heart of yours, so full of confidence, is nothing but a balloon – one little pin and it's completely deflated!

FIGARO (*furious*). But this pin is the one he picked up, mother!

MARCELINE (*recalling his own words*). Oh yes, jealousy! 'I've got my own views . . . I couldn't care less . . . if Suzanne should ever deceive me, I pardon her in advance . . . '

FIGARO (*testily*). Oh, really, mother! People speak how they feel. You take the most cold-blooded judge, make him plead his own cause, then watch him trying to expound the law! Huh, I can see now why he made such a fuss about the fireworks. Well, mother, as for my darling girl with her pins, she won't get away with it – her and her chestnut trees! If I'm near enough married to be justifiably angry, then on the other hand, I'm not so far married that I can't look for another wife, and simply fling her aside . . .

MARCELINE. Now there's a nice turn of events! Let's wreck everything for the sake of a mere suspicion. Tell me, what proof have you that it's you she's deceiving, and not the Count? Have you discovered something new about her character, that you can condemn her out of hand? Supposing she does meet him under the trees, how do you know what her intention is? What she'll say there? What she'll do there? Honestly, I thought you had more sense!

FIGARO (*kissing her hand, overjoyed*). Yes, yes, my mother's right! She's always right, always! But let's allow something for human nature, mother – it'll be worthwhile later on. We'll look into the matter before making any accusations or taking action. I know where the meeting-place is. Goodbye, mother. (*Exits.*)

MARCELINE. Goodbye. I know where it is too. Now, having put him straight, let's see what Suzanne's up to, or rather, give her a warning. She's such a pretty creature! Ah, yes – when our own self-interest doesn't set us at war with each other, we poor downtrodden women do tend to run to one another for help against these terrible, arrogant men – even if they *are* idiots! (*Exits, laughing.*)

ACT FIVE

The setting is a chestnut grove in a park; two pavilions, kiosks, or garden temples stand on either side; upstage is an ornamental glade, and downstage, a garden seat. It is dark. FANCHETTE *enters holding two biscuits and an orange in one hand, and a lighted paper lantern in the other.*

FANCHETTE. In the pavilion to the left, he said. That's this one. What if he wasn't going to come now! My little actor . . . That nasty creature in the kitchen didn't even want to give me an orange and a couple of biscuits! 'Who are they for, miss?' 'Well, sir, they're for somebody . . . ' 'Ah, we know who!' Well, so what? Just because His Lordship doesn't want to see him, does that mean he has to starve? Even then it cost me a kiss on the cheek! . . . Well, who knows? Maybe he'll pay me back.

She sees FIGARO, *who approaches to take a closer look at her. She cries out, 'Ah!', and runs off into the pavilion on her left.* FIGARO *is wearing a cloak over his shoulders, and a large hat with the brim turned down.*

FIGARO. It's Fanchette!

Enter BAZILE, ANTONIO, BARTHOLO, BRID'OISIN, GRIPE-SOLEIL, *servants and workmen.* FIGARO *peers closely at each of the others as they arrive.*

FIGARO (*fiercely*). Good evening, sirs, good evening! Are you all here?

BAZILE. All those you asked to come.

FIGARO. What's the time now, roughly?

ANTONIO (*looking up at the sky*). The moon should be up by now.

BARTHOLO. So what dark deeds are you up to, eh? He looks like a conspirator!

FIGARO (*fidgeting*). Tell me, sirs, didn't you come to the castle for a wedding?

BRID'OISIN. Of course we did.

ANTONIO. We were on our way down there, through the park, to wait for the signal for your festivities to begin.

FIGARO. Well, you won't be going any farther, sirs. It's right here, under these chestnut trees – that's where we're all going to celebrate the honourable lady I'm marrying, and the noble lord who has his own plans for her.

BAZILE (*remembering the day's events*). Ah, yes, I know what this is about. (*To the others.*) We'd better leave, if you'll take my advice. There's the matter of a rendezvous – I'll tell you about it later.

BRID'OISIN (*to* FIGARO). We'll be back.

FIGARO. Right, when you hear me calling, come running without fail, all of you. You'll see something very interesting, or my name's not Figaro.

BARTHOLO. A wise man never meddles in the affairs of the great – you should remember that.

FIGARO. I do.

BARTHOLO. They've always got the upper hand, because of their position.

FIGARO. And their devious ways, you're forgetting that. But remember also that a soft touch is at the mercy of every villain going.

BARTHOLO. That's true.

FIGARO. And also that I bear the honorable name of Verte-Allure, on my mother's side.

BARTHOLO. He's the very devil.

BRID'OISIN. He is indeed.

BAZILE (*aside*). The Count and that Suzanne of his have fixed things up without me! So, I don't care what kind of mess he gets into.

FIGARO (*to the* SERVANTS). As for you, you rascals, do as I told you and light this place up, or by God, if I get my hands on you, you'll wish you were dead! (*Shakes* GRIPE-SOLEIL *by the arm.*)

GRIPE-SOLEIL (*goes off howling*). Ow! Ooh! Damn great brute!

BAZILE (*making his way out*). God send you joy, Mr Married Man! (*They exit.*)

FIGARO (*walking up and down in the darkness, gloomily*). Oh, woman, woman, woman – you weak-willed deceiver! No creature on earth can deny its instinct – so is it yours to deceive, then? After stubbornly refusing me, when I tried to kiss her in front of her mistress – at the very moment when she's making vows to me, right in the middle of the ceremony . . . He was smiling when he read it, the villain! And me standing there like a simpleton! No, my dear Count, you won't have her – you shan't have her! Just because you're a great lord, you think you have a

great mind! Nobility, fortune, rank, position – how proud
they make you feel! And what have you done to deserve
all these advantages? Contrived to get yourself born, and
that's about it. As for the rest – you're really rather
mediocre. Whereas I . . . ye gods! Buried among the
nameless crowd, I've had to deploy more skill, more
calculation, simply to survive, than it would take to
govern the whole of Spain for a century! And you would
pit your wits against mine? . . . Wait, someone's coming!
It's her! No, it's nobody . . . The night's as dark as the
devil, and here I am playing the fool husband already,
not even half-married! (*Sits down on a bench.*) Could
anything be more bizarre than my fate? The son of God
only knows who, kidnapped by bandits, and brought up
in their ways – I get disgusted with them and run off to
find an honest profession – only to be rejected on all
sides. I study chemistry, pharmacy, surgery, but not even
the backing of a great lord can do more than put a
horse-doctor's knife in my hand! Tired of making sick
animals even sicker, I try a completely different trade,
and throw myself headlong into the theatre. Out of the
frying-pan into the fire! I work up a play about life in the
harem – a Spanish author, I fondly imagine, can poke
fun at Mohammed without too many scruples. But some
ambassador instantly complains that my verses are an
offence to the Grand Turk, to Persia, to parts of the East
Indies, the whole of Egypt, and the kingdoms of
Cyrenaica, Tripoli, Tunisia, Algeria and Morocco! So, my
play's sunk in order to please a gang of Muslim princes,
not one of whom, I daresay, can even read, and who
constantly beat us over the head, shouting 'Christian
dogs, go home!' And since they couldn't break my spirit,
they revenged themselves by abusing it. My cheeks caved

in, my time was running out – I could see the grim
reaper approaching from afar, his pen stuck in his wig.
Trembling all over, I dug deep into my resources. There
was a debate at that time on the nature of wealth, and
since one can discuss something without actually
possessing it (I was penniless, naturally), I wrote
something on the value of money, in relation to gross
national product. Next thing I find myself ensconced in a
hired carriage, watching a castle drawbridge being
lowered to receive me – whereupon I abandoned all hope
of liberty. (*He stands up.*) What wouldn't I give to get my
hands on one of those nine-day wonders, so indifferent to
all the harm they cause, after some disaster had
extinguished his pride! I'd tell him . . . I'd tell him that
idiotic stories that appear in print only become important
when you try to restrict their circulation; that unless
people are free to criticise, praise is worthless; and that
only petty minds fear petty hacks. (*Sits down again.*)
Anyway, bored with harbouring an obscure parasite, he
puts me out on the street one day, and since a man has
to eat, even though he's no longer in prison, I sharpen
my quill once more, and start asking people what's going
on. I'm told that during my economic retreat, they've
established some sort of free trade system in Madrid,
which extends even to the products of the press. And
provided I make no reference to the authorities, religion,
politics, morality, people in high places, influential bodies,
the Opera, any other theatre production, any person of
note – I'm free to publish whatever I wish, once it's been
inspected by a couple of censors! So, in order to take
advantage of this delightful freedom, I announce a new
periodical, and not wishing to step on anyone else's toes,
I call it 'The Utterly Useless Review' . Phew! A thousand

wretched scribblers rise up against me, my periodical is banned, and I'm left unemployed again! I was just about to despair, when my name came up for a position. Unfortunately, I was well qualified for the work – it required an accountant, so it was a dancer that got it. There was nothing for it but to turn to stealing, so I became a banker at faro. Well now, good sirs! I dine out everywhere, and so-called fashionable people graciously open their doors to me, keeping two-thirds of my profit for themselves, of course. I could easily have restored my fortunes – I was beginning to understand that if you want to make money, it's not what you know, it's who you know. But since people all around me were robbing each other blind, while demanding that I stayed honest, I was ruined again. So, I promptly renounced the world, and might well have put twenty fathoms of water between us, but that a beneficent God recalled me to my first profession. I picked up my bundle, and my leather barber's strop, and leaving illusions to those fools who live by them, and my pride in the middle of the road – it's too heavy for a pedestrian – went from town to town, shaving folk, without a care in the world. A great lord then comes to Seville, he recognises me, I fix him up with a wife, and as a reward for all my efforts, he's now lying in wait for mine! All kinds of intrigues and storms. And just as I'm about to fall into the abyss, and marry my own mother, my parents turn up! (*He springs to his feet excitedly.*) Heated arguments – it's you, it's him, it's me – it's none of us! Well, who is it, then? (*He falls back down again.*) A truly bizarre sequence of events! So how did all this happen to me? Why these things, and not others? Who laid all this at my door? I've been forced to take this road, unwittingly, and by the time I leave it, unwillingly, I'll have strewn it with as many flowers as my high spirits have allowed. I say my high spirits without knowing whether I have any more than other people, or even what this 'me' I'm worried about actually is: first, a shapeless collection of unidentified bits; then a mindless, puny creature; then a playful little animal; a young man, eager for pleasure, with all the tastes needed to enjoy it, plying every kind of trade in order to live; master here, servant there, as Fortune pleases; ambitious by vanity, industrious by necessity, bone idle . . . if only! Orator at a pinch, poet at leisure, musician by turns; lover in mad fits, I've seen everything, done everything, been everything. I've lost all my illusions, thoroughly disabused . . . yes, disabused! Oh, Suzanne, Suzanne, Suzanne! The torture you've put me through! Wait, I hear footsteps, someone's coming. This is the decisive moment. (*He withdraws off-stage right.*)

Enter SUZANNE *and the* COUNTESS, *dressed in each other's clothes, and* MARCELINE.

SUZANNE (*in an undertone, to the* COUNTESS). Yes, Marceline said Figaro would be here.

MARCELINE. He's here all right – lower your voice.

COUNTESS. So, one's eavesdropping on us, and the other's coming to look for me. Let's get on with it.

MARCELINE. I'll hide in the pavilion, I don't want to miss a word of this.

She goes into the pavilion where FANCHETTE *is already concealed.*

SUZANNE (*aloud*). Why, Your Ladyship's trembling! You must be cold.

COUNTESS (*aloud*). It's so chilly this evening, I think I'll go indoors.

SUZANNE. Well, if you have no need of me, ma'am, I'll take the air for a little while under these trees.

COUNTESS. You'll catch your death.

SUZANNE. I'm well wrapped up.

FIGARO (*aside*). That's not all you'll catch!

SUZANNE *withdraws to the opposite side of the stage from* FIGARO. *Enter* CHÉRUBIN *in his officer's uniform, merrily singing the refrain of his ballad.*

CHÉRUBIN.
'For I must leave my lady,
Whom I shall love for aye . . . '

COUNTESS (*aside*). It's the young page!

CHÉRUBIN (*stops*). There's someone moving – I'd better get to my hiding-place, where little Fanchette . . . It's a woman!

COUNTESS (*listening*). Oh, my God!

CHÉRUBIN (*crouches down and peers into the darkness*). Do my eyes deceive me? In this light I can just make out a headdress with feathers, and I think it's Suzanne.

COUNTESS (*aside*). What if the Count should arrive! . . .

The COUNT *appears upstage.* CHÉRUBIN *advances and takes the* COUNTESS' *hand. She tries to push him away.*

CHÉRUBIN. Yes, it's that delightful young lady who goes by the name of Suzanne! Well, now! How could I possibly mistake this soft little hand, the way it gently trembles – and not least the beating of my own heart?

He tries to place the COUNTESS' *hand over his heart, but she pulls it away.*

COUNTESS (*whispers*). Go away!

CHÉRUBIN. If it was pity that led you, on purpose, to the very spot where I'm hiding in the park . . .

COUNTESS. Figaro's coming.

COUNT (*advancing downstage, aside*). Isn't that Suzanne I see?

CHÉRUBIN (*to the* COUNTESS). I'm not frightened of Figaro. Anyway, it's not him you're waiting for.

COUNTESS. Who is it, then?

COUNT (*aside*). She's with someone.

CHÉRUBIN. It's His Lordship, you saucy creature – he asked you for this rendezvous while I was behind the chair this morning.

COUNT (*aside, furious*). It's that damned page again!

FIGARO (*aside*). And people say you shouldn't eavesdrop!

SUZANNE (*aside*). The little chatterbox!

COUNTESS (*to* CHÉRUBIN). Please remove yourself.

CHÉRUBIN. Not until I've received at least some reward for my obedience.

COUNTESS (*alarmed*). What? You're demanding . . .

CHÉRUBIN (*brightly*). Twenty kisses on your own account first, then a hundred for your beautiful mistress.

COUNTESS. And you would dare to . . .

CHÉRUBIN. Yes, of course I would! You're taking her place with the Count, I'm taking the Count's place with you. And Figaro's taken in completely!

FIGARO (*aside*). Scoundrel!

SUZANNE (*aside*). Typical page – what a cheek!

   CHÉRUBIN *tries to kiss the* COUNTESS. *The* COUNT *steps between them and receives the kiss himself.*

COUNTESS (*moving aside*). Oh, heavens!

FIGARO (*hearing the kiss, aside*). And that's the sweet young girl I was marrying!

CHÉRUBIN (*feeling the* COUNT's *clothes, aside*). It's His Lordship! (*He runs into the pavilion where* FANCHETTE *and* MARCELINE *are already hiding.*)

FIGARO (*steps forward*). I'm going to . . .

COUNT (*mistaking him for* CHÉRUBIN). Well, since you're not repeating the kiss . . . (*Aims a blow at him, which lands on* FIGARO.)

FIGARO. Ow!

COUNT. That's the first one paid for!

FIGARO (*withdraws, rubbing his jaw. Aside*). Eavesdropping has its bad points.

SUZANNE (*laughing out loud, at the other side of the stage*). Ha ha ha!

COUNT (*to the* COUNTESS, *whom he mistakes for* SUZANNE). What do you make of that page? He gets a hard slap to the face, and he runs off laughing.

FIGARO (*aside*). If somebody did that to him!

COUNT. Honestly! I can't take a step without . . . (*To the* COUNTESS.) Anyway, let's forget all this nonsense – it'll only spoil the pleasure I feel in finding you here.

COUNTESS (*imitating* SUZANNE's *voice*). Were you hoping to?

COUNT. After your ingenious little note! (*He takes her hand.*) Why, you're trembling.

COUNTESS. I was frightened.

COUNT. Just because I got one from him, doesn't mean you should be deprived of a kiss. (*He kisses her on the forehead.*)

COUNTESS. Such liberties!

FIGARO (*aside*). Shameless hussy!

SUZANNE (*aside*). Charming!

COUNT (*taking his wife's hand*). What beautiful fine skin – if only the Countess had hands like that!

COUNTESS (*aside*). Oh! I can't believe it!

COUNT. Or arms so firm and rounded? Or such pretty fingers, so graceful and mischievous?

COUNTESS (*imitating* SUZANNE). So much for love . . .

COUNT. Love is nothing but a fiction of the heart. It is pleasure that is its history, and which brings me now to your feet . . .

COUNTESS. You no longer love her?

COUNT. Yes, I do very much, but after three years together, marriage seems so respectable!

COUNTESS. What did you want from her?

COUNT (*caressing her*). What I have found in you, my lovely . . .

COUNTESS. Tell me.

COUNT. I don't know. More variety, perhaps. More bite – a certain kind of charm, difficult to define – the occasional rebuff . . . I really don't know. Our wives think all they have to do is love us. Once that's settled, they simply go on loving us – non-stop! That's if they *do* love us. And then they're so ready and willing, so eager to please – always, constantly – that one is rather surprised, one fine day, to find boredom, where one looked for contentment.

COUNTESS (*aside*). What a lesson!

COUNT. In truth, Suzanne, it's often occurred to me that if we men seek elsewhere the pleasures which elude us at home, it's because our wives don't pay enough attention to the art of sustaining our interest, of reawakening our love, of reviving, so to speak, the charm of possession with that of variety.

COUNTESS (*stung*). So it's all up to them?

COUNT (*laughing*). And nothing to do with the men? Can we change nature's way? Our task is to win them; theirs is to . . .

COUNTESS. Theirs?

COUNT. Is to keep us. People too often forget that.

COUNTESS. Well, I certainly shan't.

COUNT. Nor I.

FIGARO (*aside*). Nor I.

SUZANNE (*aside*). Nor I.

COUNT (*taking his wife's hand*). We're getting an echo here –
let's keep our voices down. Anyway, you needn't worry
about such things, you whom love has made so pretty
and full of life. With just a dash of whimsy, you'll be the
most teasing of mistresses.(*Kisses her on the forehead.*) My
Suzanne, a Castilian's word is his bond. Here is the gold
I promised to buy back the right I no longer possess over
that delicious moment you have granted me. But because
the grace with which you do so is beyond price, I am
adding this diamond to it, which you shall wear for love
of me.

COUNTESS (*curtseying*). Suzanne graciously accepts.

FIGARO (*aside*). Could she be more brazen?

SUZANNE (*aside*). This gets better and better.

COUNT (*aside*). That's caught her interest – so much the
better!

COUNTESS (*looking upstage*). I can see torches.

COUNT. It's your wedding party. Shall we go inside one of
these pavilions a moment, and let them pass?

COUNTESS. Without a light?

COUNT (*gently leading her away*). What for? We've nothing to
read.

FIGARO (*aside*). Good God, she's going in! I might have
known! (*He comes forward.*)

COUNT (*turning round, in a loud voice*). Who goes there?

FIGARO (*angrily*). I'm not going, I'm coming!

COUNT (*to the* COUNTESS, *in a whisper*). It's Figaro! (*Takes
to his heels.*)

COUNTESS. Wait for me!

She runs into the pavilion to the right, while the COUNT *disappears among the trees upstage. In the darkness,* FIGARO *strains to see where they have gone, still believing that the* COUNTESS *is* SUZANNE.

FIGARO. I can't hear a thing now. They've gone in, and that's that. (*In an altered voice.*) You foolish husbands, who employ spies, and spend months in pursuit of a suspicion without ever running it to ground, why don't you follow my example? Right from the start, I'm following my wife and eavesdropping on her. In an instant, I know what's going on. It's perfect – no more doubts, I know exactly where I stand. (*Quickens his pace.*) Happily, I'm not in the least concerned, her betrayal leaves me quite unmoved. But now I've got them at last!

SUZANNE (*who has crept downstage in the darkness, aside*). You'll pay for those suspicions of yours! (*Imitating the* COUNTESS' *voice.*) Who goes there?

FIGARO (*dismayed*). Who goes there? Someone who heartily wishes he'd been strangled at birth!

SUZANNE. Why, it's Figaro!

FIGARO (*peering at her, nervously*). Your Ladyship!

SUZANNE. Please, don't shout.

FIGARO. Oh, my lady, Heaven has brought you here at just the right moment. Where do you think His Lordship is?

SUZANNE. What do I care? He's an ungrateful wretch. Tell me . . .

FIGARO. And Suzanne, my fiancée – where do you think she is?

SUZANNE. Not so loud, please!

FIGARO. That Suzanne, whom everyone believed so virtuous, who pretended to be so modest! They're shut up in there together! Listen, I'm going to call . . .

SUZANNE (*clapping her hand over his mouth, and forgetting to disguise her voice*). No, don't!

FIGARO (*aside*). God dammit, it's Suzanne!

SUZANNE (*in the* COUNTESS' *voice*). You seem a little anxious.

FIGARO (*aside*). Traitor! She's trying to trick me.

SUZANNE. We must have our revenge, Figaro.

FIGARO. Is that what you truly desire?

SUZANNE. I wouldn't be true to my sex if I didn't. However, you men know hundreds of ways . . .

FIGARO (*confidently*). We all have our part to play, my lady. And the women's way is by far the best.

SUZANNE (*aside*). I'll give him a good thump!

FIGARO (*aside*). It would quite funny if before the wedding . . .

SUZANNE. But what kind of revenge is it, if it's not spiced up with a little love?

FIGARO. Ma'am, you may have no inkling of it, but that's because it's hidden by respect for your position, believe me.

SUZANNE (*stung*). I don't know if that's what you really think, but it's not a nice thing to say.

FIGARO (*comically feigning passion, on his knees*). Oh, my lady, I adore you! Just think of the time, the place, and the circumstances, and may your resentment make up for any deficiency of grace in my plea!

SUZANNE (*aside*). My fists are itching!

FIGARO (*aside*). My heart is pounding!

SUZANNE. But, sir, have you considered? . . .

FIGARO. Yes, my lady, I have considered.

SUZANNE. That when it comes to love and anger . . .

FIGARO. . . . He who hesitates is lost. My lady, your hand.

SUZANNE (*in her own voice, giving him a slap*). There you are!

FIGARO. Ow, you little devil! What a slap!

SUZANNE (*slapping him again*). What slap? This one?

FIGARO. What's that for? Dammit to hell, are you beating carpets or what?

SUZANNE (*hitting him at each phrase*). Hah! What's that for? It's for me, Suzanne! And that's for your suspicions, that's for your revenge, that's for your treachery – for your nasty tricks, and your insults, and your little schemes! Is this the kind of love you were talking about this morning? Well, is it?

FIGARO (*stands up, laughing*). Holy Saint Barbara! Yes, yes, it's love! Oh, joy! Oh, bliss! Oh, Figaro – a hundred times happy Figaro! Hit me again, my darling, don't let up! But when you've covered my body with bruises, look on me kindly, Suzanne – the luckiest man ever beaten by a woman!

SUZANNE. The luckiest man! You scoundrel, that didn't stop you trying to seduce the Countess, all those phoney sweet nothings, to the point I almost forgot myself – I was actually giving in to you on her behalf!

FIGARO. Now, could I really mistake your lovely voice?

SUZANNE (*laughing*). You mean you recognised me? Oh, I'll have my revenge yet!

FIGARO. What, give me a good hiding and still bear a grudge? That's a typical woman! But do tell me how I happen to find you here, when I thought you were with him, and why these clothes, which deceived me, now prove your innocence.

SUZANNE. What? It's you that's the innocent, walking right into a trap laid for someone else. Is it our fault, if we try to muzzle one sly fox and catch two?

FIGARO. Who's caught the other one, then?

SUZANNE. His wife.

FIGARO. His wife?

SUZANNE. Yes, his wife!

FIGARO (*wildly*). Oh, Figaro, you deserve hanging! Imagine not guessing that! His wife? Ye gods, the sheer deviousness of women! So, those kisses I heard . . .

SUZANNE. Were given to Her Ladyship.

FIGARO. And the page, Chérubin's?

SUZANNE. To His Lordship.

FIGARO. And earlier, behind the settee?

SUZANNE. To nobody.

FIGARO. You're sure about that?

SUZANNE (*laughing*). You're asking to get slapped again, Figaro.

FIGARO (*kissing her hand*). That'll be something to treasure. The Count's was a different matter, though – he meant it.

SUZANNE. What! Down on your knees, you arrogant creature!

FIGARO. Serves me right! On my knees, head bowed, grovelling, I prostrate myself before thee . . . (*Does so.*)

SUZANNE (*laughing*). Oh, dear – the poor Count! What a lot of trouble he's gone to . . .

FIGARO (*getting up onto his knees*). To seduce his own wife!

The COUNT *appears upstage and goes straight to the pavilion on the right.*

COUNT (*to himself*). I can't find her anywhere in these trees – perhaps she's gone in here.

SUZANNE (*to* FIGARO, *in a whisper*). It's him.

COUNT (*opening the pavilion door*). Suzanne, are you in there?

FIGARO (*whispering*). So, he's looking for her, and I thought . . .

SUZANNE (*whispering*). He didn't recognise her.

FIGARO. Well, shall we finish him off? (*Kisses her hand.*)

COUNT (*turning round*). What! A man on his knees to the Countess! Hah! And I've no weapon . . . (*Comes downstage.*)

FIGARO (*springing to his feet, and speaking in an assumed voice*). You will forgive me, my lady – I hadn't realised that our regular rendezvous would clash with this wedding . . .

COUNT (*aside*). It's him! It's the man in the dressing-room this morning! (*Strikes himself on the forehead.*)

FIGARO. Still, never let it be said, eh? We shan't allow a silly obstacle like that to stand in the way of our pleasure.

COUNT (*aside*). Murder! Death! Hell and damnation!

FIGARO (*leading* SUZANNE *towards the pavilion, whispers*). He's swearing. (*Aloud.*) So, let's hurry, my lady, and make up for what we missed when I had to jump out of the window.

COUNT (*aside*). Aha! It's all out in the open at last.

SUZANNE (*near the pavilion at left*). Better make sure no-one's following us, before we go in. (FIGARO *kisses her on the forehead.*)

COUNT (*cries out*). Vengeance!

SUZANNE *runs into the pavilion where* FANCHETTE, MARCELINE *and* CHÉRUBIN *are already concealed. The* COUNT *catches hold of* FIGARO *by the arm.*

FIGARO (*feigning terror*). It's my master!

COUNT (*recognising him*). What! You scoundrel, it's you! Help! Help! Somebody!

PÉDRILLE (*entering in his riding boots*). My Lord, I've found you at last!

COUNT. Thank God, it's Pédrille. Are you alone?

PÉDRILLE. I've just got back from Seville, riding like a fiend.

COUNT. Right, come here, and shout at the top of your voice!

PÉDRILLE (*does so*). Couldn't find the page anywhere! Here's the commission!

COUNT (*pushing him away*). You idiot!

PÉDRILLE. But Your Lordship told me to shout.

COUNT (*still holding on to* FIGARO). For help, you fool. Help, somebody! If you can hear me, anybody – help, come quickly!

PÉDRILLE. But there's two of us here, sir – Figaro and me. What more do you want?

BRID'OISIN, BARTHOLO, BAZILE, ANTONIO, GRIPE-SOLEIL, *and the entire wedding party run on, carrying torches.*

BARTHOLO (*to* FIGARO). You see? As soon as you gave the signal . . .

COUNT (*pointing to the pavilion at left*). Pédrille, guard that door! (PÉDRILLE *goes to do so.*)

BAZILE (*to* FIGARO, *in a whisper*). Did you catch him with Suzanne?

COUNT (*pointing to* FIGARO). And the rest of you, my loyal servants, surround this man! Guard him with your life!

BAZILE. Ha, ha!

COUNT (*furious*). Be quiet! (*To* FIGARO, *in an icy tone.*) Now, my bold cavalier, will you answer my questions?

FIGARO (*coolly*). How can I refuse, my lord? You're in control of everything here, except yourself.

COUNT (*restraining himself*). Except myself?

ANTONIO. That's telling him!

COUNT (*losing his temper again*). No, if there's one thing guaranteed to make me even angrier, it's that damn cool manner he puts on.

FIGARO. What, are we soldiers, to kill or be killed, for causes we know nothing of? Personally, I like to know what I'm angry about.

COUNT (*enraged*). This is madness! (*Controlling himself.*) Very well, sir – you claim you know nothing. Fine, then perhaps you would be so kind as to tell us exactly who that lady is, whom you've just taken into the pavilion?

FIGARO (*mischievously, pointing to the other pavilion*). What, that one?

COUNT (*testily*). No, this one!

FIGARO (*coolly*). Oh, I see. That's a young lady who honours me with a particular show of affection.

BAZILE (*astonished*). Ha, ha!

COUNT. You hear that, gentlemen?

BARTHOLO. We do indeed!

COUNT (*to* FIGARO). And this young lady – has she any other obligations, to your knowledge?

FIGARO (*coolly*). I do know that a certain great lord was interested in her for a time, but whether he's abandoned her, or whether she simply finds me a more attractive proposition – anyway, she's made her preference known.

COUNT (*angrily*). Preference . . . ! (*Controlling himself.*) At least he's open about it. He admits his guilt, gentlemen, and I swear to you I've heard the very same, out of the mouth of his accomplice.

BRID'OISIN (*stunned*). His accomplice!

COUNT (*in a fury*). Well, now – since the dishonour has been made public, the vengeance must be also. (*Goes into the pavilion.*)

ANTONIO. That's only right.

BRID'OISIN (*to* FIGARO). So, which one's taken the other's wife?

FIGARO (*laughing*). I'm afraid no-one's had that pleasure.

COUNT (*speaking inside the pavilion, dragging out someone as yet unseen*). It's a wasted effort, Madame – the game's up, your hour has come! (*He emerges, without looking round.*) Fortunately, this detestable union hasn't yet been blessed . . .

FIGARO (*exclaims*). Chérubin!

COUNT. My page?

BAZILE. Ha, ha!

COUNT (*enraged, aside*). That damned page, always! (*To* CHÉRUBIN.) What were you doing in that pavilion?

CHÉRUBIN (*timidly*). I was keeping out of your sight, sir, as you told me to.

PÉDRILLE. So I've ruined a good horse for nothing!

COUNT. Antonio, go in there and bring her out for judgment – bring out the shameless creature who has dishonoured me.

BRID'OISIN. Is it Her Ladyship you're looking for?

ANTONIO. It'll serve you right. You've done plenty of that yourself . . .

COUNT (*furious*). Get in there, dammit! (ANTONIO *enters the pavilion.*) You will see, gentlemen, that the page was not alone.

CHÉRUBIN (*meekly*). My fate would have been too cruel, had there been no kind heart to sweeten its bitterness.

ANTONIO (*pulling someone out, as yet unseen, by the arm*). Come on, ma'am, there's no point in making me beg you to come out – we all know you went in there.

FIGARO (*calls out*). My little cousin!

BAZILE. Ha, ha!

COUNT. Fanchette!

ANTONIO. God's blood! This is too much! His Lordship picking me to show everybody it was my own daughter that caused all this trouble!

COUNT (*enraged*). How was I to know *she* was in there? (*Makes to go in himself.*)

BARTHOLO (*stepping in front of him*). If you will allow me, Your Lordship . . . This is all very confusing. I'm quite calm . . . (*He goes in.*)

BRID'OISIN. This is a very complicated affair.

BARTHOLO (*bringing out* MARCELINE). Have no fear, my lady, nobody's going to hurt you, I promise. (*Turns round and exclaims.*) Marceline!

BAZILE. Ha, ha!

FIGARO (*laughing*). This is madness! My mother's in it too?

ANTONIO. Worse luck, yes.

COUNT (*enraged*). Who cares! It's the Countess . . . Ah, here she comes now!

SUZANNE *emerges, concealing her face behind her fan. The* COUNT *seizes her roughly by the arm.*

Well now, gentlemen, what do you think she deserves, eh? This disgusting . . .

SUZANNE *falls to her knees, head bowed.*

COUNT. No, no!

FIGARO *falls to his knees, at the other side.*

COUNT (*louder*). No, no!

MARCELINE *falls to her knees before him.*

COUNT (*still louder*). No, no!

The entire company kneel down, with the exception of BRID'OISIN.

COUNT (*beside himself*). I don't care if there were a hundred of you!

The COUNTESS *now emerges from the other pavilion and falls to her knees.*

COUNTESS. Then at least let me be one of them.

COUNT (*staring at the* COUNTESS *and* SUZANNE). Eh? What's this I see?

BRID'OISIN (*laughing*). Good God, it's Her Ladyship.

COUNT (*attempts to lift her to her feet*). What? Was it you, Countess? (*In a pleading voice.*) Only the most generous and forgiving . . .

COUNTESS (*laughing*). You'd say, 'No, no!', if you were in my place. However, for the third time today, I forgive you unreservedly. (*She stands up.*)

SUZANNE (*stands up*). Me too.

MARCELINE (*stands up*). Me too.

FIGARO (*stands up*). Me too. There must be an echo round here! (*Everyone stands.*)

COUNT. An echo! I tried to make fools of them, and they've treated me like a child.

COUNTESS (*laughing*). Don't feel sorry about it, my lord.

FIGARO (*dusting off his knees with his hat*). A day like this is good training for a diplomat.

COUNT (*to SUZANNE*). What about that letter, fastened with a pin?

SUZANNE. Her Ladyship dictated it to me.

COUNT. So, the reply rightly goes to her. (*Kisses the COUNTESS' hand.*)

COUNTESS. Everyone shall have what is due to them. (*She gives the purse to FIGARO and the diamond to SUZANNE.*)

SUZANNE (*to FIGARO*). Another dowry!

FIGARO (*slapping the purse in his hand*). And of the three, this was hardest to get hold of!

SUZANNE. Like our marriage.

GRIPE-SOLEIL. And the bride's garter – may I have it?

The COUNTESS pulls out the ribbon, which she has been keeping in her bodice, and throws it to the floor.

COUNTESS. The garter? It was inside her dress – there it is.

The young men make a rush for it. CHÉRUBIN *is first on the scene.*

CHÉRUBIN (*snatching it up*). If anyone wants this they'll have to deal with me!

COUNT (*laughing, to* CHÉRUBIN). For someone so touchy, tell me – how did you enjoy that smack on the jaw you got recently?

CHÉRUBIN (*stepping back, half-drawing his sword*). *I* got, sir?

FIGARO (*mock-indignant*). It was my jaw he got it on! That's how great men dispense justice.

COUNT (*laughing*). *You* got it? Ha, ha, ha! What do you think of that, my dear Countess?

COUNTESS (*her mind elsewhere, recovers herself and answers fervently*). Yes, indeed, my dear, and for the rest of my life, I do assure you.

COUNT (*slapping* BRID'OISIN *on the back*). And what do you think, my dear Brid'oisin? What's your verdict?

BRID'OISIN. On everything I've seen here, my lord? Truly, I don't know what to tell you. And that's my judgment.

ALL. Well delivered!

FIGARO. I was poor and people despised me. I showed some spirit, and their hatred intensified. Now, with a pretty wife, and some money . . .

BARTHOLO (*laughing*). People will flock to you in droves.

FIGARO. Is that possible?

BARTHOLO. I know what they're like.

FIGARO (*to the onlookers*). Leaving aside my wife and my fortune, you will do me the honour, I trust . . .

The orchestra begins to play, and all join in the singing and dancing.

BAZILE.
Triple dowry, lovely wife,
Fortune smiles on married life!
At noble lord, or beardless page
Only jealous fools would rage.
The ancients' words we comprehend –
A keen wit triumphs in the end!

FIGARO. I know . . . (*Sings.*)
Let the well-born rejoice!

BAZILE. No. (*Sings.*)
Let the well-found rejoice!

SUZANNE.
Should a wanton husband stray,
He brags of it, 'tis seen as play,
But let his wife attempt the same,
She faces infamy and shame –
Rough justice, surely, and the cause?
'Tis men alone who make the laws!

FIGARO.
The jealous husband, foolish man,
To keep his wife safe, if he can,
Sets a fearsome dog to guard
His honour and patrol his yard.
Come night, alas, he'll soon discover,
The dog bites all except the lover!

COUNTESS.
>One's of independent mind,
>To husband's faults no longer blind;
>Another, on the point of sin,
>Swears she loves no-one but him.
>Least foolish is the wife who cares
>For nought except her own affairs!

COUNT.
>Country women, rustic beauties,
>Forever mindful of their duties,
>Will surely scarce repay your pains.
>Just give me a wife with brains!
>Like the lucky coin ne'er spent,
>She's a blessing, heaven sent!

MARCELINE.
>The gentle mother, as we say,
>Brings us forth to greet the day.
>All the rest, through heaven above,
>Remains the mystery of love.

FIGARO.
>The mystery's how such a one
>Could produce a handsome son!

>Fate maps out our lives on earth,
>King or shepherd, at our birth.
>Merest chance determines which,
>But wit alone can make us rich.
>Let majesty parade its crown,
>Voltaire will cast the tyrant down!

CHÉRUBIN.
>Lovely ladies, gossamer light,
>Give us many a sleepless night,

Though we curse your very name,
We must love you, just the same.
As actors feign to scorn the pit,
Yet strain each nerve to conquer it!

SUZANNE.

Should within this merry work
Some worthy moral lesson lurk,
Thank reason, not our witty lines,
For even so wise Nature signs
The path that leads to life's true treasure –
Appealing to our need for pleasure!

BRID'OISIN.

Now, sirs, our little play is ended,
And to your judgment here commended.
Faults apart, we've tried to show
How people blithely come and go
Till some great man does them wrong –
Then they sing a different song!

Curtain.